# SYLVIA PORTER'S A HOME OF YOUR OWN

*Other Avon Books by*
**Sylvia Porter**

SYLVIA PORTER'S 442 TAX-SAVING TIPS
*(1989 Edition)*
SYLVIA PORTER'S LOVE AND MONEY
SYLVIA PORTER'S NEW MONEY BOOK FOR THE 80'S


*Coming Soon*

SYLVIA PORTER'S YOUR FINANCIAL SECURITY
SYLVIA PORTER'S 478 TAX-SAVING TIPS
*(1990 Edition)*

# SYLVIA PORTER'S A HOME OF YOUR OWN

## Sylvia Porter

**With the Contributors to <u>Sylvia Porter's Personal Finance Magazine</u>**

AVON BOOKS ◆ NEW YORK

This book is intended to provide general information. The publisher, author, and copyright owner are not engaged in rendering personal finance, investment, tax, accounting, legal, or other professional advice and services and cannot assume responsibility for individual decisions made by readers. Should assistance for these types of advice and services be required, professionals should be consulted. References to tax provisions in this book are based on current tax laws and regulations. Revisions in tax law, if adopted, might affect the tax consequences.

SYLVIA PORTER'S A HOME OF YOUR OWN is an original publication of Avon Books. This work has never before appeared in book form.

AVON BOOKS
A division of
The Hearst Corporation
105 Madison Avenue
New York, New York 10016

Copyright © 1989 by Davis Publications, Inc.
Published by arrangement with Davis Publications, Inc.
Library of Congress Catalog Card Number: 88-91350
ISBN: 0-380-89755-5

First Avon Books Trade Printing: April 1989

AVON TRADEMARK REG. U.S. PAT. OFF. AND IN OTHER COUNTRIES, MARCA REGISTRADA, HECHO EN U.S.A.

Printed in the U.S.A.

OPM   10   9   8   7   6   5   4   3   2

# Acknowledgments

Thanks are extended to the following authors for permission to reprint part or all of their articles from *Sylvia Porter's Personal Finance* magazine:

Joseph Anthony, "A Custom-Tailored Mortgage"
Warren Boroson, "Whose Side Is Your Real Estate Agent On?"; "The Remodeling Option"
Suzanne Chazin, "Move or Remodel?"
Patricia Schiff Estess, "Buying a Home with Family Help"
Marilyn Larkin, "Smart Moves"
Lucinda L. McCartney, "Before You Do Anything"
Ruth Rejnis, "If Your Dream Home Has Problems..."
Alan Rosenthal, "Insuring Against Floods"
Mark Stevens, "So You're About to Go to a Closing..."
Stanley Zarowin, "Security Systems for Your Home"

# Contents

# Chapter 1

# The Case for Buying Rather Than Renting

Your home. It's an extension of yourself, a source of self-esteem and identity—as well as a secure place to dine, sleep, and entertain.

Your home is also very likely the most expensive purchase you'll ever make, and therefore a step that you must take with the utmost of caution and thought. Your house may be the cornerstone of your financial plans: If you need money in an emergency—to pay unexpected medical bills, for example—you can borrow against your house. Or you can borrow to help send your children through college, or to help yourself start a new career, or launch a well-researched business.

Finally, your house is also an investment—one that appreciates nicely in normal times, one that soars in inflationary times. And if you bought a good home for a good price in a good location, and you maintained it properly, you're almost guaranteed to sell it for a handsome profit. When you decide to retire, you might sell your home, move to smaller accommodations, and use your profit to make your golden years more comfortable.

Ask any financial planner what a young couple should do after they've made sure they have enough health, disability, and life insurance, and after they've built up an emergency cash-reserve fund. The answer almost always is: Buy a house.

## Buying Versus Renting

At one time the difference between renting a home (or apartment) and owning a home was minimal.

You bought if you wanted to put down roots, or if you preferred the privacy of living in your own home, or if you simply wanted independence. In your own home, you could paint the walls whatever color you want, or install an exercise room—if that's what appealed to you—knowing that, when you sell, you would retrieve some of your expenditure simply by raising your offering price. You could also have pets, and pay no attention to the restrictions you used to encounter in leases. Besides, you would almost certainly have more space in a home of your own than you'll get in rented quarters.

On the other hand, you would rent for the sake of fewer responsibilities (your landlord must make repairs and improvements) and more flexibility (it's far easier to pack up and leave rented quarters than to sell a house).

Whatever course you chose made little difference financially. The long-term price appreciation that you reaped from owning a house was more or less offset by the cash you had tied up in the down payment (the lump sum you must fork over to obtain a mortgage), plus home-maintenance costs, the expense of amortization (paying the interest on your mortgage and repaying the principal), and the property taxes. Still, if you chose the more carefree life of just renting, you emerged with zero profit when you moved.

What happened to make owning a house so much smarter, financially?

Inflation, for one thing.

Real estate and other hard assets (gold and precious metals) appreciate spectacularly during inflationary times—and do fine during ordinary times.

Even during a recession, real estate doesn't do as poorly as other investments—like stocks.

If you ask home owners what they paid for their houses 10 or 20 years ago, and what they could sell them for now, you may be in for a shock. Houses that people bought for $30,000 may be worth $300,000. (See the table at the end of this chapter.)

## Uncle Sam Loves Home Owners

Another reason owning your own residence is so profitable is that Uncle Sam loves a home owner. You can deduct your mortgage interest payments and your local property taxes. (And, in the early years, those mortgage interest payments make up the bulk of your monthly payments.) You can borrow against your house, and deduct all the interest on up to $100,000. On top of all that, your profits when you sell your house may be postponed—or forgiven altogether (up to $125,000).

There are other tax benefits, too. If you use a room (or just a section) of your home to conduct a business, you can deduct the cost of heating and maintaining that room as an expense. You can reduce any income you receive from your business by these costs. You can even deduct them from your income if your business earns no profit in two out of every five years. You merely have to show that the room was essential to your business, and you used it for nothing else.

If you rent out your house, you get another wonderful tax benefit as well: depreciation. While your house is undoubtedly growing in value, for tax purposes you can deduct its supposed drop in value year after year. And you can deduct the cost of your repairs the year after you make them.

True, the overall tax benefits of owning your own home have been curtailed somewhat. That's because tax rates have dropped. A deduction is worth more when the highest tax rate is 50 percent than when it's 28 percent (or 33 percent).

Even so, any deduction is worth more than no deduction. And those other tax breaks for home owners —like the postponement of taxes on your profits —remain. What other investment can you make that exempts $125,000 of your profit from taxes? (For more about the tax aspects of home ownership, see Chapter 20.)

And let's not forget other financial benefits, such as your recapturing some of the cost of any improvements you make to the house when you sell—whether it be the addition of a room, a remodeled kitchen, an extra bathroom, or improvements that just make your house look better, like attaching beams to the ceiling. Later on in the book, we'll tell you which additions are the most likely to pay off when you sell.

## The Affordability Factor

Unfortunately for Americans buying their first houses, it's far more difficult today than it used to be.

David O. Maxwell, chairman and chief executive officer of the Federal National Mortgage Association, recently told the National Association of Home Builders:

> There are those who deny that affordability is a problem for first-time home buyers. They argue that the run-up in home values has benefited the

parents of young, potential home buyers, and eventually the higher housing value will be passed along.... That argument is based on the myth that the typical first-time home buyers in America are the Yuppie offspring of well-to-do parents, waiting for Dad and Mom to retire to a condo in Orlando or Scottsdale.

In fact, the people we're talking about are policemen, hairdressers, office and factory workers, families with two incomes who can't afford to buy a house near their jobs.

In constant dollars, family income remained flat from 1973 to 1984. But housing prices rose sharply. The median-priced home now absorbs nearly twice as much family income as it did in 1973. That is why this decade has seen the first decline in our rate of home ownership in 50 years. And that decline has been most pronounced among the age groups that buy first homes.

Later in this book, we'll explore some ways even not-well-to-do Americans can buy homes—such as by borrowing from their parents or relatives, or sharing home ownership with friends.

## Who Shouldn't Buy

No, we're not saying that everyone should buy a home.

In order to meet the mortgage payments, the property taxes, the repairs and maintenance, you need a steady income. In other words, you or your spouse, or both of you, should have secure jobs. You'll also need savings—to make the down payment (typically 20 percent of the purchase price), to cover closing costs (like bank and lawyer's fees), to buy new furniture, and to deal with emergencies.

You should be planning to live in the home for at least two years. Otherwise, the costs of buying and selling the house will erase any profits you might make—and perhaps even wind up costing you money. If your job requires you to move often, it may not be worth the time, effort, and cost to find a home, arrange to finance it, and then have to pay brokers and lawyers to sell it again.

A new home owner, ideally, will know something about home repair and maintenance. If you must call in a plumber whenever there's a leak in a faucet, or if you don't know why your windows should be properly caulked (to prevent heat from escaping in winter, and keep in air-conditioned air during the summer), the financial benefits of home owning will begin to vanish.

You must also be willing to keep your house in good shape. This means more than just gardening, snow shoveling, leaf raking, and lawn mowing. It means tending the furnace, replacing broken shingles, draining the water heater, replacing leaky gutters. The more a house is neglected, the more damage will be done, and the more costly the eventual repairs and maintenance will be.

You also should know when, and whom, to ask for help. A great many novice home owners, for example, don't know enough to hire a home engineer before making the most expensive purchase of their lives. Or how to find knowledgeable, helpful real estate agents and lawyers.

In short, ideal first-time home owners have (a) a steady source of income; (b) enough saved to make a down payment, without exhausting money they may need for emergencies; (c) the expectation of remaining in the same area for a few years; (d) the willingness to keep a house in good running order; and (e) the willingness to learn about buying and selling a house.

* * *

This book will advise you on buying, maintaining, improving, protecting, and selling your home. We'll show you how to get the best for less money, the most for the fewest hassles, and the highest return for the lowest investment.

Yes, buying a home can be intimidating. And some people make disastrous mistakes—buying in deteriorating communities, or choosing homes that are unbearably hot in summer, unbearably cold in winter, with flooded basements and leaking roofs.

But you can avoid most of the perils if you simply do your homework.

And this should be one of your chief textbooks.

### The Difference That 10 Years Make
### Typical Home Prices in Various Parts of the Country

| Area | 1977 | 1987 | % Change |
|------|------|------|----------|
| USA | $44,000 | $ 95,000 | +116 |
| San Francisco | 72,000 | 169,347 | +135 |
| Los Angeles | 65,000 | 142,900 | +120 |
| NY–NJ Metro | 48,500 | 142,400 | +194 |
| Washington, DC | 68,000 | 137,500 | +102 |
| Minneapolis | 47,250 | 114,000 | +141 |
| Chicago | 50,900 | 110,000 | +116 |
| Baltimore | 47,000 | 106,500 | +127 |
| Philadelphia | 45,000 | 99,000 | +120 |
| Columbus | 42,000 | 88,000 | +110 |
| St. Louis | 37,000 | 84,600 | +129 |
| Miami | 48,500 | 78,900 | + 63 |
| Milwaukee | 42,900 | 76,400 | + 78 |
| Houston | 46,900 | 73,000 | + 56 |
| Portland | 35,500 | 72,950 | +105 |
| Pittsburgh | 37,800 | 71,500 | + 89 |

Source: U.S. League of Savings Institutions.

# Chapter 2

# Coming to Terms

A real estate *broker* acts as an intermediary between the buyers and the sellers, showing property to prospective buyers and negotiating purchase contracts. For this, the broker charges the seller a percentage (usually 5 to 7 percent) of the selling price of the property as his or her commission. A broker has his or her own office, and must have passed a licensing test.

A broker who is a member of the National Association of Realtors, one of the most powerful trade organizations in the country, is a *Realtor.*

A real estate *agent* can be either a broker or someone who works for a broker—usually the latter. Agents receive part of a commission if they *list* a house (accept the original assignment of selling it), and another part of a commission if they find a "ready, willing, and able" buyer. They share their commissions with their brokers.

Once buyers find that special house, they enter into a preliminary agreement (a *binder*) with the seller and pay a small amount of money *(earnest* money) for the right to buy the property on the agreed-upon terms. The binder usually has *contingency* clauses, making the sale dependent upon the results of an inspection of the property and the buyer's getting a mortgage agreement from a lender.

This *mortgage* is the money you borrow to buy a house, using the house as *collateral*. In other words, a mortgage is the written legal claim on the real estate of the person buying the property. Collateral represents the assets you put up as security for the payment of the money you borrowed.

If the buyer cannot repay the money he or she owes the lending institution (the buyer *defaults*), the lender can have the property sold to meet the debt. This is known as a *foreclosure*.

Before a mortgage agreement is entered into, an expert must make an *appraisal* of the property. The appraiser, who may be a broker, estimates the current market value of the property—what it would probably sell for.

Mortgage lenders—including banks and savings and loan associations—may charge borrowers *points* to raise the yield on their loans, thus lowering the interest rate they charge. A point is 1 percent of the amount of the mortgage loan. One point on a $65,000 mortgage is $650.

Mortgages are usually either *fixed-rate* or *adjustable-rate mortgages* (ARMs). With a fixed rate, the interest rate is unchanging. With an adjustable, it bobs up and down, depending upon an outside indicator—like the rates on six-month Treasury securities. The more desirable ARMs have *caps*—limits on how much the interest rate can rise over a mortgage's term, and how fast it can rise over a specified period of time.

When the borrower pays back the mortgage loan, he or she typically does it in installments—typically, once a month. This method, called *amortization,* reduces the debt gradually. The money you borrowed is the *principal*. You pay back both the principal and the interest in the same payment. In the earlier years of a mortgage, your payments go mainly toward the interest. (A fuller list of mortgage terms appears at the end of Chapter 6.)

There are numerous extra costs to buying property, over and above the purchase price. These *closing* costs may include lawyers' fees, insurance, and taxes. (The word "closing" can also mean persuading a buyer to sign a contract. Agents have all sorts of ways to "close" a buyer—such as mentioning all the other supposed buyers who are allegedly interested in a particular house.)

Buyer and seller meet at the closing—the formal end of the transaction, when the *deed* changes hands. The buyer gives the seller payment for the property and, in return, receives the deed—the legal document that transfers the ownership of a property from one person to another. A deed is usually available for public inspection in a town's *recorder's* office. Once you have a deed, you have *title* to the property.

Any money or documents handed over to a third party, to hold in reserve, is held in an *escrow* account. If you put down a deposit on a house, it's held "in escrow."

If you repaint the outside of your house, it's a *repair*. But if you spend a lot of money altering your house, such as by adding a new room, it's an *improvement*. This distinction is important for tax purposes. Home owners who don't rent out their property can subtract the cost of improvements from the profits when they sell, but not the cost of repairs.

Your *basis* is what you spend for the house. That includes not just the purchase price, but legal fees and the cost of improvements. A good synonym: total investment.

The *offering* price is what you want to sell your

house for. The *selling* price is what you actually sell it for. Let's hope that, in your case, they're the same.

Some other terms:

**Acceleration Clause:** A provision in a mortgage that allows the lender to demand immediate payment of the balance of a debt—for example, if the borrower is late on payments. Not desirable for home buyers.

**Condominium:** A residence in which each unit is owned by an individual, rather than by an overall landlord, and in which the unit owner has part ownership of common areas, like hallways.

**Cooperative:** An apartment house owned by all the residents, usually as shareholders in a nonprofit corporation, and managed by an elected board of directors. Not as popular as condominiums.

**Creampuff:** A desirable house in a desirable location.

**Easement:** A right that an individual or company has to use someone else's property—for example, to use your house's driveway to get access to his/her own property.

**Equity:** The amount of money a home owner has in a property, beyond a mortgage or other obligations.

**Fizzbo:** A home owner selling a house without a broker, thus trying to avoid paying a commission. From the initials of "For Sale By Owner" (FSBO).

**Graduated Payment Mortgage:** A mortgage in which a young buyer starts off with low payments, which gradually grow higher—as the buyer's income supposedly increases. Such mortgages can be dangerous to both mortgagor and mortgagee.

**Handyman's Special:** A house that has deteriorated and needs a great deal of repair work.

**Lease-Option:** A prospective buyer lives in the seller's house and pays rent, but has the right to buy the house in the future. The rental payments may go toward the house's purchase price.

**Lien:** A legal claim on a property for payment of a debt.

**Mechanic's Lien:** A claim against land and buildings brought by workers who haven't been paid for their labor or materials.

**MGIC:** Mortgage Guaranty Insurance Corporation, the largest seller of private-mortgage insurance. Lenders may require buyers who cannot afford a 20 percent down payment to pay extra for private-mortgage insurance.

**Personal Property:** Anything not permanently attached to a house, like freestanding bookshelves. When a house is sold, personal property usually doesn't go with it.

**Prorate:** To divide financial obligations proportionately. If a seller has paid a year's taxes in advance, for example, the cost will be prorated with a buyer.

**Qualify a Buyer:** To check into a potential buyer's financial ability to buy a property.

**Real Property:** Land and anything permanently attached to it.

**Right of First Refusal:** A buyer's right to match a third party's bid for property.

**Sump Pump:** A pump, usually in a house basement, that automatically disposes of groundwater.

**Survey:** A map of a tract of land showing its size, boundaries, and such.

**Tenancy in Common:** A form of ownership in which each owner has an undivided interest in the property. If one owner dies, his or her interest goes to his/her heirs, not to the other tenants in common.

**Tenants by the Entirety:** A form of ownership, particularly between husband and wife, in which the surviving spouse automatically takes title when the other spouse dies.

**Time Is of the Essence:** A phrase in a contract stipulating that the terms must be fulfilled by a certain date.

**Title Insurance:** Insurance against the loss of ownership of all or part of a property because of a defect—such as the previous owner's spouse not having signed the contract of sale.

**Trust Deed:** A deed that the seller conveys to a third party, to be held in trust until the buyer fulfills certain obligations.

**Variance:** An exception made to a community's zoning ordinances. (See below.)

**Zoning Ordinances:** A community's rules governing the use of land.

# Chapter 3

# Deciding What
# You Can Afford

Can you afford to buy a house? It depends upon your savings, your regular income—and the price of the house you have in mind.

There's a quick-and-dirty rule: You can afford a house selling for two to two-and-a-half times your family's gross income minus your long-term debts (such as for a car you bought on time). Most of the time, the fraction will be closer to two than to two-and-a-half. If the house you have in mind costs $90,000, you ideally will have a net income of $45,000. We're assuming that you can afford a 20 percent down payment: $18,000.

What if your net income is only $36,000 or less? Try to boost your down payment. Lenders may be more welcoming; you yourself will have lower mortgage payments to make.

Another way of calculating what you can afford: Your expenses for your house shouldn't exceed 28 to 33 percent of your monthly income. (Lenders have a lot of leeway—hence the range between 28 and 33 percent.)

Let's say that your monthly income is $3,000, or

$36,000 a year. You want an $80,000 house. For the 30-year mortgage you're seeking, you would pay $600 a month. You'll also pay real estate taxes—in your area, perhaps 1.5 percent of the house price ($100 a month). For insurance, 0.5 percent ($33 a month). For utilities, 3 percent ($200). For maintenance, 1 percent ($66).

Total monthly housing expenses: around $1,000. (We're overlooking the fact that the mortgage interest and real estate taxes are deductible.)

Now divide the $1,000 by your monthly income: $3,000. Result: 33 percent.

You're at the borderline. Lenders may think hard about providing you with a mortgage. And you might consider buying a less expensive house—or asking your employer for a raise—or somehow boosting your down payment.

By applying the first rule—a house should be two to two-and-a-half times your net income—you can see that a $36,000 income means you can afford a $72,000 to $90,000 house.

But before deciding what price house you can afford, talk to local lenders. Find out the standards that they use for granting mortgages in your particular area. If you can get an FHA-insured mortgage, you can probably qualify for a more expensive house.

After you've decided whether you can afford to buy a house, and the price you can pay, you'll need a financial statement. This is simply a summary of your assets, your debts, and your sources of income.

Once you have your statement, you're ready to apply for financing as soon as you find the right house. This can give you an advantage over someone who might be competing for the same property, because bankers look fondly on loan applicants who come prepared with a businesslike inventory of their assets and liabilities. It's also a powerful tool for persuading sellers that you're worthy of favorable terms —not just a reduction in the offering price, but a move-in day that meets your convenience, along with your getting the appliances and furnishings included in the selling price.

Typically a financial statement comes in two parts: a balance sheet composed of your assets and liabilities, which shows your net worth; and an income/expense statement, which gives a picture of your cash flow.

A financial statement might include a special section for information about your family. Mention your credit cards, your insurance, the fact that you've never failed in business or compromised debts with your creditors, that there are no suits or judgments pending against you, and that you have a recent will on file with your lawyer.

Use a looseleaf notebook as a binder for your papers, so you can easily update your financial statement every three or six months, or when your financial picture changes (e.g., you switch jobs, or shift investments). Better still, if you have a personal computer, enter in it all the information. Updating then becomes a snap.

# Chapter 4

# Choosing What's
# Best for You

Once you're armed with a financial statement, you
and your family should decide what you want in the
way of a house. Where? What price? A condominium
or a cooperative? An old house or a new one? How
many bedrooms? A large plot, for recreation and privacy, or a small plot, for less maintenance? One garage or two—or more?

Do you want a Colonial (a two-story)? A ranch
house (one story)? A Tudor or Elizabethan (a slate
roof, timbers imbedded in the walls)? A Cape Cod
(one-and-a-half stories)? How about a split-level?

## Styles in Houses

In general, two-story houses may be best for young
families. The children can be sleeping upstairs while
you're entertaining downstairs. Heating and cooling
costs will be lower. On the other hand, you'll have lots
of stair-climbing. And you should install an escape
ladder for the second floor, in case of a fire.

For older people, a one-story means less stair-climbing—but also more expenses. A one-story is more expensive to build (it requires a large lot, roof, and foundation), more expensive to maintain (if the roof needs repair, it's a major outlay). But it's easy to clean. And the transition from indoor to outdoor living is easy.

With a split-entry, you climb up or down stairs as soon as you enter. The basement gets lots of light, because it's relatively high—and may collect less moisture than typical basements. But you'll be going up and down stairs a lot, and you may find it hard to keep the basement at one temperature.

With split-levels, you enter into the living area. A short flight of steps down leads to the social area; a short flight up, to the bedrooms. This is an especially good design for a sloping lot.

Cape Cods have low heating costs, but the second-floor rooms may be small. If the attic has been turned into bedrooms, the house may be too cold in winter, and too warm in summer, because of inadequate insulation.

Tudors are striking, but such houses—because of their angles—may be hard to heat and cool evenly.

## The Best Location

All right, it's time to repeat the old cliché: The three most important criteria in choosing a house are location, location, and location.

The cliché bears repeating because it's so easy to choose a house in a bad location. A house in lower Podunk will probably cost much less—and probably have more bedrooms, a bigger plot, brick siding instead of frame, lower taxes, and so forth.

The trouble is, such a house will appreciate less: Buyers want to live in upper Podunk, which has better schools, bigger parks, more efficient services, and cleaner and safer streets. (That's what the higher taxes pay for.) You may also prefer the neighbors in upper Podunk to those in lower Podunk.

## Old or New?

Also decide in advance whether you want a new house or an older one. New houses cost more, but usually have modern appliances, superior plumbing and electrical systems, better insulation, and whatever else is fashionable these days, like fireplaces and kitchen dining nooks. Old houses give you more of a selection—there are 50 times as many of them—and usually they're better located (near schools and shopping). Also, they probably were built more carefully, with superior materials.

Judy and Tom Striver fell in love with a Mediterranean charmer built in the 1920s. The home was spacious, with beautifully proportioned rooms, floor-to-ceiling windows, and a living room with beamed ceilings and a massive stone fireplace.

It also had inadequate wiring, an old inefficient kitchen, bathrooms that needed remodeling, and an unreliable heating system. The windows throughout needed caulking or reputtying. Indeed, except for a coat of fresh paint, the house had simply not been kept up by its current owners, a couple in their late 80s.

Nonetheless, the young couple bought it—for some $20,000 less than comparable houses were bringing. They intended to renovate it slowly.

But before they could start on the kitchen or wiring, they found themselves facing astronomical heating bills that ate into their remodeling savings. From the first winter on, they were in a holding pattern, using money they had thought would put their house in order to pay for emergency repairs.

They never got to the point where they could enjoy the house completely. Instead, it seemed to be a Damoclean sword perpetually hanging over their heads, threatening financial disaster. And the house, which might have become a gracious showplace, remained a white elephant.

The phrase "white elephant" is an apt description of this condition: In olden times, the King of Siam (now Thailand) would give a subject who displeased him a sacred white elephant. The care and upkeep of the animal was mandatory, and its requirements could bankrupt the owner.

Not all old homes are white elephants, nor are all white elephants bad buys. But Judy and Tom committed the single most dangerous error that buyers can make when they were lured by the charm of their Mediterranean "elephant." They forgot that "Investigate before you invest" is a maxim that holds true for more than stocks and bonds.

True, the young couple had hired an engineer to inspect the home, and he had highlighted the problems. But they thought that the $20,000 they were saving—and would be able to apply to remodeling— would take care of all the repairs. Their calculations were about $50,000 too low.

Contrast Judy and Tom with the Whites. Greg and Jean also wanted an older home for their three children and for Jean's mother, who lived with them. They also found a "handyman's special"; but many of the repairs needed in the Tudor they wanted were ones that Greg, who was skillful with tools, could handle. Greg knew he could fix and replace most of the exterior plumbing in the bathrooms, and he had the patience and time to repair squeaky floors, and even to replace windows.

What he couldn't do was replace the cast-iron pipes that were originally installed as waste lines. The estimate he got for that job ran $4,000; he added another $4,000 for windows, $2,000 for painting, and $5,000 for sinks, bowls, and tiling for two bathrooms. All told, he expected to have to shell out some $15,000 to $18,000 in the first year to make the house habitable. The kitchen would have to wait several more years.

With those estimates, he decided to get a larger mortgage to free up cash for the work. And he set a work schedule for both himself and the plumbing contractor, so that he had some time to enjoy the house during that first year.

As cautionary as these tales are, they don't mean you have to settle for a mouse if you can't refurbish an elephant. Older houses don't necessarily have these problems. Some are kept up wonderfully well, and when they are, they often offer a charm not found in more modern houses. Although you're likely to pay top dollar for a sound one, you might find an out-of-favor home for less. It may be badly decorated, lack closets or a lavatory on the main floor, or just look tired. Before you make any choice of an older home, you had best examine it with a critical eye—and with the help of experts.

*New* houses can be a joy, too. Being the first to live in one, though, brings some extra costs you ought to figure on. First, the windows: Unless your house was built with combination windows, you'll probably want to add storms and screens immediately. Next, you'll probably have major expenses for landscaping, although builders typically seed lawns and may put in a bush or two near the front door. Of course, carpeting

and draperies or window shades, which usually stay
with an older home, won't be found in a new one.
Don't look for built-ins, either. Anything in the way of
bookshelves are extras in a new home.

You'll also have to go through the shakedown cruise
blues. Doors stick or don't close properly; roofs leak;
appliances don't work. If your lawyer has protected
you properly when you bought the new house, these
early difficulties must be repaired free of charge by
the contractor—usually after some frustration in getting him or her to send a crew back.

## Co-ops and Condos

There are other choices out there. If you're not wed-
ded to the idea of living in a private house, consider
cooperative apartments and condominiums. Here are
some issues to consider:

As an owner of a cooperative, you'll be able to afford
far more in services than you can as a private home
owner, because you're sharing costs with all the other
stockholders. On the other hand, your maintenance
costs usually are at the mercy of the board of directors, who can raise them for repairs or for added
amenities at their own discretion. Boards can even insist that any sales of cooperative apartments be for
cash only, which means that buyers cannot obtain
mortgages, but must, for example, sell assets to come
up with the total price.

If such rules seem unreasonable and arbitrary to
you, think twice before buying into a cooperative. Indeed, courts have held that boards of cooperatives can
wield almost dictatorial powers. In the event you
want to sell your apartment, they can refuse to accept
your buyer, no matter how sound, for any reason they
choose. In some New York City apartment coopera-

tives, prestigious and wealthy lawyers have been turned down as buyers simply because they might be more litigious than other tenants.

As a cooperative member, you're required to continue paying maintenance costs and any mortgage outstanding, until you find a buyer acceptable to the board. If you don't, the board can evict you, because your shares entitle you only to rent your apartment. And you'll still be responsible for the costs of that apartment.

You'll typically have less trouble when you buy into a condominium, which is treated as your own home by the courts. But there is another problem. The property you own in common with all the other tenants costs money to maintain. You're charged a monthly fee, which can go up sharply if there are vacancies in the building. Then, too, condo owners usually are assessed periodically for any major repairs to common property or for roofs and exterior painting.

Condos have another drawback: It's sometimes difficult to get satisfaction from other tenants who may damage your property, either inadvertently or carelessly. For example, you might have to call your own plumber to find a grout leak in your neighbor's condo, then end up in court suing him or her for your damages. Such petty annoyances make for uncomfortable living arrangements, but they are not unusual.

Around the country there are new types of condos going up that have many of the advantages of private houses with some of the pluses of group ownership. These condos consist of private houses, complete with all facilities, including small plots of land that are part of the ownership package. Lawn work and snow shoveling are handled by a home-ownership association that contracts out the management of the development. Except for the fact that these units, because they have no common walls, are more expensive to build and to heat, they sometimes are the best bet for young couples or retirees.

## Is a Prefab for You?

Remember the story of the three little pigs? One built his house of straw, one of wood, and one of bricks. Well, you don't have to build your own house out of bricks today to keep the wolf from the door. In fact, you would do better to build your own house from a prefabricated kit. That is so much less expensive than hiring contractors, architects, and builders that you're almost guaranteed to keep the wolf at bay.

Can you really build your own house, though? You'd better believe it. And you're likely to come out with a better home than if you were to farm the job out. But there are a few things to consider:

1. Do you honestly like to work with your hands? You don't need artisan skills, but you do have to know the business end of tools and have the ability to read blueprints.
2. Have you the time? Once the house is framed, you must work steadily to enclose it, or the interior may suffer from the weather.
3. Do you know your own limitations? You must be willing to call in professionals when a task is beyond you. Another limitation: your patience. Are you likely to get tired of spending every weekend on it, and rush the job through at the end?
4. Can you understand and follow the building code in your area sufficiently well to get a certificate of occupancy (c/o) when the house is completed? Generally, building codes cover electrical work,

plumbing, basic construction, sanitation systems, and fire-retardant materials. You'll need
the c/o from the local inspector to move in, and
you'll need it as well if you want to get a mortgage when the house is finished.

If you decide to build your own home, also consider
factory prefabricated homes. You'll have a wide variety to choose from. They include:

**Precut** homes: These are what are usually referred
to as "kit homes." Typically, kit homes form only the
bare-bones shell, with no plumbing, heating, or electrical work.

**Modular** or **sectional** homes are factory-built, and
include all fixtures and appliances as well as flooring,
paneling, and such. These are more expensive than
the kit homes and can cost several hundred thousand
dollars. Typically these units require skilled builders
to put together, although once they are set up, you get
more amenities per square foot.

**Panelized** homes: These are a cross between precut
and modular units, and can offer more than the
former but usually less than the latter. Choose these if
your skills are limited.

**Manufactured** homes are really mobile homes, de-
livered to a building site and reassembled there.
Often several units are put together for larger homes.

Many companies are in the business of manufactur-
ing homes. You'll need to take the same precautions in
buying one that you'd need with any other major purchase. Check out the manufacturer with the Better
Business Bureau. Ask to see other homes in your area
that have come from the company. Talk to the owners
about the problems they've had, how they've been re-
solved, and what they would have changed if they had

to do it over. Find out how much of the home they were able to build themselves, and how much it cost to call in specialists.

Prefabricated houses can be bought for as little as $15,000 but can cost as much as several hundred thousand. And the house and land alone are only part of your costs. You'll need excavation for a basement or a foundation of some sort—and if the ground isn't level or is particularly rocky, you might even need some detonating to clear it. A water supply is essential, either from city lines or a well (which must be dug). You'll need either sewer lines or a septic-tank system, and utility line hookups. The more remote your site is, the more these will cost, because you'll have to pay not only for transportation of all materials to the site but for time and material.

Finally, you ought to have a good idea of how you will finance the home. Typically, when you build a house, you get a construction loan paid to the builder in steps, as the house progresses. But with a kit home, you've got to pay for the materials when they arrive. So your loan has to be up front. The kit manufacturer might be able to help you get the loan—or if you hire a general contractor for part of the work, he or she can also be of help.

You might use your land as collateral for the initial loan. Once the home is built, though, you could well be able to mortgage it for more than it costs. The bank will appraise it and assess it against comparable homes in the area.

Now that you've made overall decisions—what you can afford, where, what style of house you want, whether new or used—you're ready to go shopping.

Don't fall for a pretty face. A house may have lovely flowers and charming awnings and a gurgling brook out back. But don't neglect such mundane matters as how close you want your house to be to public transportation, to churches or synagogues, to shopping and recreation.

On a similarly unromantic level, keep in mind that brick houses need less maintenance than frame houses—but cost more. Corner houses may compromise privacy—and give you two lengths of sidewalks to sweep and clear of snow.

Be wary of a house on a steep hill: Bicycling may be out, and walking may be difficult. In wet weather, even driving may be unsafe. A house on the bottom of a hill, similarly, may collect water in the basement.

If a house is on a busy street, it may be dangerous for young children. If it's next to a busy street, drivers may use it to avoid congestion on the main street.

Make sure to check the area within a half-mile for noisy, smelly factories and deteriorating houses.

Be wary of buying the most expensive house in your area: When you want to resell, buyers in your neighborhood will be looking for typical houses, not expensive ones. Buyers who could afford your house may be looking in a more well-to-do community.

In shopping for a house, you may find it helpful to narrow down your choices. Otherwise you may exhaust yourself, spending weekend after weekend checking out every house available. Decide, perhaps, that you want an old Colonial for $80,000 in a quiet area, near a particular school, and close to shopping and public transportation.

But don't be too picky. If you don't like the colors of a house, or the wallpaper inside, you can change them. And you may even wind up with a house more expensive than you planned to pay, or a Tudor instead of a Colonial. Perfect houses are rare. Be willing to compromise.

*  *  *

At this point, you can begin the exhilarating part of house hunting: checking newspaper advertisements, looking at bulletin boards, and driving around looking for houses for sale. And now you will need a journal. Use it to describe every house you look at, the price, the location, the pluses and minuses. (See the following checklist.)

Some real estate authorities suggest that you see at least ten properties before you make your first offer. That way, you'll get a feel for the properties available, and be able to judge whether particular prices are unusually high or low.

You'll probably have the widest selection of houses in the early spring. Home owners want to sell in the summer, so their children can start school at the beginning of the fall. If you buy during the winter, the selection may be small, but you might get the best bargains, simply because you won't have that much competition. Buyers like to buy in the spring, too.

## Neighborhood Inspection Checklist

**Neighborhood quality**                                      **Yes**  **No**
1. Are the homes well taken care of?                            ☐       ☐
2. Are there good public services (police, fire)?              ☐       ☐
3. Are there paved roads?                                       ☐       ☐
4. Are there sidewalks?                                         ☐       ☐
5. Is there adequate street lighting?                          ☐       ☐
6. Is there a city sewer system?                               ☐       ☐
7. Is there a safe public water supply?                        ☐       ☐
8. Are the public schools good?                                ☐       ☐

**Neighborhood convenience**
1. Will you be near your work?                                 ☐       ☐
2. Are there schools nearby?                                   ☐       ☐
3. Are there shopping centers nearby?                          ☐       ☐
4. Is there public transportation available?                  ☐       ☐
5. Will you be near child-care services?                       ☐       ☐
6. Are hospitals, clinics, or doctors close by?               ☐       ☐
7. Is there a park or playground nearby?                       ☐       ☐

**Neighbors**
1. Will you be near friends or relatives?                      ☐       ☐
2. Will you be near other children of your kids' ages?         ☐       ☐
3. Will you feel comfortable with the neighbors?              ☐       ☐
4. Is there an active community group?                        ☐       ☐

**Does the neighborhood have any problems, such as:**
1. Increasing real estate taxes?                               ☐       ☐
2. Decreasing prices of homes?                                 ☐       ☐
3. Lots of families moving away?                               ☐       ☐
4. Heavy traffic or noise?                                     ☐       ☐
5. Litter or pollution?                                        ☐       ☐
6. Factories or heavy industry?                                ☐       ☐
7. Businesses closing down?                                    ☐       ☐
8. Vacant houses or buildings?                                 ☐       ☐
9. Increasing crime or vandalism?                              ☐       ☐

**What is your overall rating**        **Good**  **Fair**  **Poor**
**of the neighborhood?**                 ☐         ☐         ☐

Courtesy, U.S. Department of Housing and Urban Development.

## Comparing Houses

| | 1 | 2 | 3 |
|---|---|---|---|
| Address | | | |
| Asking price | | | |
| Real estate taxes | | | |
| Water bill | | | |
| Heating bill | | | |
| Electric bill | | | |
| Age of house | | | |
| One-story | | | |
| Two-story | | | |
| Split-level | | | |
| Wood frame | | | |
| Brick | | | |
| Aluminum siding | | | |
| Exterior condition | | | |
| Storm windows | | | |
| Garage/capacity | | | |
| Gas heat | | | |
| Electric heat | | | |
| Hot-water heat | | | |
| Age of plant | | | |
| Central air/age | | | |
| Bedrooms | | | |
| Size of living room | | | |

Courtesy, Chicago Title Insurance Company.

## Comparing Houses

| | 1 | 2 | 3 |
|---|---|---|---|
| Dining room | | | |
| Kitchen | | | |
| Number of bathrooms | | | |
| Closets/size | | | |
| Refrigerator/age | | | |
| Stove/age | | | |
| Disposal/dishwasher | | | |
| Clothes washer/dryer | | | |
| Laundry space | | | |
| Water heater | | | |
| Basement storage area | | | |
| Finished basement | | | |
| Attic storage area | | | |
| Finished attic | | | |
| Number of fireplaces | | | |
| Drapes | | | |
| Carpeting | | | |
| Modern electrical wiring | | | |
| Sump pump/drainage | | | |
| Public sewer system | | | |
| Backyard patio | | | |
| Fence on lot lines | | | |
| Pleasing landscaping | | | |

## Comparing Condo or Co-Op Units

|  | 1 | 2 | 3 |
|---|---|---|---|
| Address |  |  |  |
| Asking price |  |  |  |
| Real estate taxes |  |  |  |
| Monthly assessment |  |  |  |
| Utility bill |  |  |  |
| Square footage |  |  |  |
| Storm or thermal windows |  |  |  |
| Central or individual air-conditioning/age |  |  |  |
| Smoke detectors |  |  |  |
| Number of bedrooms |  |  |  |
| Number of bathrooms |  |  |  |
| Separate dining room |  |  |  |
| Kitchen eating area |  |  |  |
| Closets—number and size |  |  |  |
| Refrigerator/age |  |  |  |
| Cooking stove/age |  |  |  |
| Disposal/age |  |  |  |
| Dishwasher/age |  |  |  |
| Balcony and/or patio |  |  |  |
| Double entry |  |  |  |
| Drapes |  |  |  |
| Carpeting |  |  |  |

Courtesy, Chicago Title Insurance Company.

# Chapter 5

# Borrowing from Family, Co-Owning with Friends

One-third of all houses purchased by first-time home owners are now bought with the help of a relative. No wonder. With the average house selling for $90,000 to $100,000, and the average 30-year-old college graduate earning in the mid-20s, it's almost impossible for the first-home buyer to amass the $19,000 needed for a 20 percent down payment.

Thank heaven for parents, grandparents, aunts, and uncles.

Before accepting help from your parents or other relatives, have them examine their financial situations. "Under no circumstances should parents deplete their cash or emergency reserves," warns Inga H. Hanna, a certified financial analyst in Portland, Maine.

Make sure your parents do some long-range projections before they make any decisions. You must feel confident that they'll continue to be in good health and that they'll have a steady stream of income for many years. Once they make a large gift or loan to you, it's tucked into the bricks, and will be hard for you to pull out without your disrupting your own financial foundation. Says Hanna, "Wouldn't it be a shame if generous parents were to discover that they have to forgo early retirement because their financial cushion is lining their child's home?"

Then, too, you must reflect upon who has control. Will your parents be content to offer sound advice, while leaving the decision making to you—since, after all, you're actually going to live in the house?

Here are a few tips for parents from Lynne Clark, a broker with the Van Wert Agency in Scarsdale, New York (you might ask them to read this chapter):

- Parents should let their children do the shopping. But they should give their children a basic list of what to look for and what questions to ask.
- If parents feel that they must approve the final choice of house before they hand over any funds, they should know what constitutes a bargain in today's terms. "The house they remember being on the market for $20,000 'just a few years ago' is now a staggering $250,000," Clark says. "Rather than have these horrified parents kill the purchase at the last moment because they're out of touch with the home market, I encourage them to come along on the house-hunting marathon to get a feel for the market. Then, when a son or daughter makes the final selection, the parents will be more confident that the home has value in today's market."

As for you, the beneficiary of this generosity, you should ask yourself:

- Are you mature enough to accept money, or advice, without feeling that your independence is being threatened?

- Can you openly disagree with parental advice without feeling guilty or upset? Might you go along with a parent's advice even if you vehemently disagree—like buying a rundown shack in an older part of town, for rock-bottom price?
- Will the money that you're receiving lower your parents' standard of living?
- Would you be as conscientious about repaying a loan from a relative as one you received from a bank?

Parents have a variety of ways to help their children become home owners:

GIFTS    Says Mari Mennel, a New York City financial planner, "If it's possible, and if parents would like to pull out money from their estates for tax purposes, I always suggest an outright gift of money rather than a loan. It's the best 'no strings' way to transfer money." They can give away a hefty chunk of cash without gift-tax consequences: $10,000 per person per year. If a father and a mother want to make a gift to both their son and daughter-in-law (or daughter and son-in-law), they could bestow as much as $40,000, tax-free.

LOANS    Any loan should be an "arm's-length" transaction, set up according to the usual legal rules—how much interest will be charged, when payments are due. That way, the child-borrower can deduct the interest. Even if the parent-lenders don't charge any interest, the IRS will consider that they did—and tax them on their "phantom" income.
    The one break for parents is that the IRS will let them lend $100,000 or less interest-free, provided the

borrower doesn't have investment income of more than $1,000 a year, notes Jeffrey Cogas, an accountant in Huntington, New York.

One way for parent-lenders to survive this psychological mine field is to make it clear (by written records) that any unpaid loans will be treated as "advancements," reducing the child-borrower's share of the parent's estate. Would-be lenders and would-be borrowers also should be aware of the power elements that can intrude ("calling in" a demand note if the child-borrower gets a divorce, for instance). They should work hard to make the lending decision on the basis of financial factors, and a desire to help—not on a sense of guilt, or a desire to control.

For a businesslike loan, keep these factors in mind:

- The borrower should be ready to show that he or she can make the monthly payments, and that the interest rate is competitive with other investments open to the lender.
- Adequate collateral can reassure the lender. Of course, the borrower must understand that the lender can legally seize the collateral if the loan isn't paid, risking a family feud to do this.
- As a rule of thumb, set the interest rate halfway between what the lender would receive from a safe investment and what the borrower would pay for a comparable bank loan.
- As with any business deal, this one should be supported with adequate documentation. You'll need an exchange of letters, with the lender specifying the loan amount, when the money will be turned over, the repayment schedule, and the interest rates. The borrower should agree to these terms in writing. A formal loan note (plus security agreement, if the borrower provides collateral)

may be even better. Buy the forms at a stationery store, and get a lawyer's advice in filling them out.

Because of the close relationship that Kathy Scozzare and her husband, Anthony Paonita, have with Kathy's parents, they were able to devise an arrangement that combined the best features of outright giving and lending.

"Kathy's parents graciously gave us $37,000 for the down payment on a three-family home in Staten Island, New York," Anthony relates. "We earn enough now—Kathy's a second-grade teacher, and I'm a lawyer turned journalist—that we can save substantial sums. We had a verbal agreement to repay them over a five- to ten-year period."

Says Joseph Scozzare, Kathy's father, who plans to retire from Procter & Gamble in a few years: "It works well. They'll be able to use the money now, and we'll have it back when we need it for retirement."

COSIGNING A MORTGAGE    Cosigning is not the innocuous gesture it may seem. It means that the borrower can get a mortgage with no cash down. But it's perilous for the cosigner. If the borrower defaults on the mortgage payments, the cosigner is 100 percent liable.

Sidney M. Moskowitz, a real estate lawyer in New York City, gives parents this advice: "Before you cosign a mortgage agreement, insist that it contain a provision whereby you must receive, by certified or registered mail, a duplicate of any late-payment reminder or default notice sent out to your relative. Although it doesn't relieve you of liability, it will make you aware of what's happening in time to speak to your relative about correcting the situation."

Something else parents must consider when they

cosign: They must disclose that liability on any subsequent financial statement they fill out, which means that their own borrowing power may be curtailed. Suppose that they want to buy a vacation home in addition to their primary residence. When they apply for a mortgage, the lender may limit or even turn down their request because their potential debt seems excessive.

EQUITY SHARING   If the parents want tax deductions, they and their offspring might consider a shared-equity arrangement. Example:

A couple earn enough money to cover monthly mortgage payments and maintenance on a $150,000 house. But they don't have the cash for the $30,000 down payment. The husband's father agrees to spring for most of the down payment in return for half-ownership of the house.

The two sets of owners will split monthly mortgage costs, taxes, and insurance. The couple are responsible for maintaining the house they live in (painting, mowing the lawn, etc.). The couple pay the father a fair-market rental on his share, and the IRS allows them to take the same deductions allowed to any home owner: half the mortgage interest and real estate taxes.

The father can also claim deductions for his half of the mortgage interest and taxes—although the rental income from the couple will offset most of those deductions. And he can go a step further. As an owner of rental property, he can also take a deduction for depreciation of the building and his share of the operating costs (such as insurance).

If you go the route of equity sharing, handle it as a strictly-business transaction. Duane Gomer of Mission Viejo Center, California, who conducts real estate seminars, gives this advice:

- Have a contract reviewed by a lawyer. Make certain that it clarifies who is responsible for maintenance, how long the shared-equity arrangement will last, and how to deal with problems (what happens if the owner-residents want to sell, for example).
- Make sure that the house is readily marketable. It should be in a good location, and be in apple-pie order, so that it can be rented quickly if the resident-owners must move.
- The resident-owners should contribute to the down payment, even if their contribution is small. Says Gomer, "That financial commitment makes it more difficult for the resident-owner to walk away from the investment, and less likely that the property will be neglected."

Up to now, we've been talking about borrowing money from relatives, or even friends, to make a down payment. But there's another course if you don't have enough money: Buy a house with friends, or even just acquaintances.

Joint home ownership by people who aren't related remains untraditional. But if handled correctly, it allows two partners—or even more—to reap the full benefits of a home at only half the cost.

Many banks actually welcome mortgage applications from unrelated partners. And why not? With two names on the application, there's twice as much chance that the loan will be paid off.

Look for a partner in similar circumstances, with similar needs. If you have kids, match up with another family. Or if you're single, find another single. Look for someone who expects to spend about the same amount of time and money on the place as you do. And make sure the two of you are compatible. If you're fastidious, beware of a slob. If you like peace and quiet, beware of someone who likes loud music and raucous parties. If you're accommodating, steer clear of someone who's stubborn. If you're conscientious—you won't take advantage of another person—avoid someone who thinks he or she is always entitled to the lion's share.

Work out the rules in advance. If it's a weekend, or vacation, home, will you use the house together, or on alternate times of year? Are certain parts of the house off-limits to the other partner?

Some people have found it useful to draw up an informal contract setting out their rights and responsibilities, and describing how they will handle a breakup:

- If one partner dies, the 50 percent ownership of the house passes to that partner's heirs, not to the other partner.
- All mortgage, tax, insurance, and utility payments are split down the middle, regardless of who uses the place more.
- All improvements must be okayed by both partners, and the cost split 50–50. Any improvements ordered by only one partner must be paid solely by that partner.
- If one partner wants out, he or she sets a price for half of the ownership. The other partner, within a prearranged deadline, then decides whether to buy at that price. (Or the contract can call for an appraiser, mutually agreed-upon, to set the price.)
- Either partner can sell his or her 50 percent share to a third party, providing that the other partner approves. If one partner vetoes a third-party sale but declines to match the offer, the entire property is to be listed at fair market value, and sold, with the partners' splitting the proceeds.

The most important unwritten rule is courtesy. Each partner must be willing to give in when the other expresses a strong preference—whether it be for an improvement, or for fewer raucous parties.

# Chapter 6

# Mortgages Made Easy

For the four million Americans buying some version of the American dream this year, finding the right home is only half the challenge. The other half is finding the right mortgage.

The wild assortment now available complicates the hunt, but also makes it easier for astute shoppers to get the right loan. Think of looking for a mortgage as being similar to looking for a new outfit: The myriad variations on what you want may be daunting, but it almost guarantees you'll find something suitable. And somewhere, somehow, there's a mortgage tailored for your financial shape. The usual 30-year, fixed-rate loan with 20 percent down is too stiff and unyielding for you? Don't despair—you can almost certainly find something more comfortable to slip into.

Here's a look at some well-tailored options for people in various financial conditions.

## Where to Shop

The seller is your first stop. Find out whether you can take over the seller's existing mortgage. With an assumable mortgage, you may be able to acquire all, or a portion, of your financing at a below-market in-

42

terest rate. In addition, you usually don't have to pay expenses linked with acquiring a new mortgage.

"I had signed a contract on a condominium I really wanted," says Carol Stacey, a computer programmer and divorcée in Overland Park, Kansas. "But I had to back out because, when I applied for a mortgage, I got turned down. Before our divorce, my husband and I had owned a house and had credit cards jointly. The story changed when I went out on my own. To the banks, it was as if I had no credit record at all.

"I was able to get the condo I live in now only because it had a freely assumable mortgage. I had money for the down payment, and I simply took over the previous owner's mortgage, which had 25 years left on it."

Another avenue to explore is whether the seller is willing to provide financing. This practice is known as "taking back a mortgage," and the mortgage is called a "purchase money" mortgage. The seller grants you a loan for the purchase price of the house, less your down payment. You obtain the title to the property and make regular payments to the seller.

Drawback: Purchase money mortgages are usually for 5 to 15 years, with a 25- to 30-year payout. This means that, instead of paying at a rate that would wipe out the mortgage within the 5- to 15-year life of the mortgage, you would fork over monthly payments as if you had a 25- to 30-year mortgage. (These payments are, of course, lower.) Then, at the end of the agreed-upon time, you must either come up with the balance in a "balloon" payment, or refinance the balance.

Like an assumable mortgage, you don't have to pay loan origination fees with a purchase money mortgage, and you avoid the delays, sometimes extending for months, that can occur with regular mortgages. What's more, the seller will usually accept a lower in-

terest rate—typically 1 to 3 percentage points below
market rates.

Sometimes you can combine a purchase money
mortgage with a mortgage assumption. Let's say that
you assume an existing mortgage, but it doesn't cover
the entire purchase price. In that case, you can try to
obtain a new loan from the seller to cover the balance.

If seller financing and mortgage assumption aren't
viable options, it's time to shop for a new mortgage.
You local newspaper may publish the rates that various lenders are offering. Check into:

- *Savings and loan associations.* S&Ls are the na-
  tion's largest mortgage lenders.

- *Commercial banks.* Because commercial banks
  aren't primarily mortgage lenders, they may not
  be competitive in rates and terms. But your employer's commercial bank may give you a special
  break.

- *Credit unions.* Most credit unions concentrate on
  short-term credit loans, but some will grant
  longer-term mortgages.

- *Mortgage bankers.* These are private companies
  that originate loans, then sell them to long-term
  investors. They are simply the middlemen for investors who want to collect mortgage interest.
  But they may be the only way you can get certain
  government-backed loans—mortgage bankers in
  general are more willing to deal with government-backed loans than are S&Ls.

  *Note:* Mortgage bankers are not the same as
  mortgage brokers. Brokers simply bring borrower
  and lender together, for a set fee. A banker actually services the account. Because brokers take
  more risks, they're likely to offer you shorter-
  term mortgages and stiffer rates.

- *Loans backed by the Federal Housing Administration or Veterans Administration.* More about these beginning on page 46.

## Mortgages: An Introduction

Once upon a time, there were just fixed-rate mortgages. You obtained a mortgage at, say, 9 percent for 30 years, and that 9 percent never changed. Everyone was happy. Except—when interest rates climbed— the lenders.

Interest rates rose in the 1970s, at one point reaching 18 percent. And the banks found themselves stuck with mortgages set at rates of only 5 percent, 6 percent, and 7 percent. To prevent this from happening again, the lenders developed new mortgage instruments, with interest rates that bob up and down with prevailing rates.

These "adjustable-rate" mortgages (ARMs) are, obviously, not nearly as desirable—from your point of view—as fixed-rate mortgages in inflationary times, when interest rates shoot up. But to make ARMs more enticing, lenders now offer them at rates that start below the rates of fixed-rate mortgages. They also put "caps" on them—limiting how much they can rise over the life of the loan, and how much they can rise over shorter periods.

Which is better, fixed rate or adjustable rate? As a general rule, choose the fixed rate—you'll know from month to month, from year to year, what you will have to pay. And if rates plummet, you can refinance the mortgage. An exception: If you plan to live in a house for only a few years, you might opt for an ARM, simply to benefit from its initial lower interest rate. But these days, the decision is even more complicated: There are now mortgages that you can switch from adjustable to fixed. (We'll have more to say about the various types of mortgages later on.)

What else should you look for in a mortgage besides
a low interest rate? The term you want—15 years, 30
years, or whatever. No prepayment penalty—which
means that if you pay off the loan early, because (say)
you're selling the house, you won't be hit with a few
hundred dollars to recompense the bank for its paperwork.

Also, with a fixed-rate mortgage, try to avoid a
"due-on-sale" clause, which would require you to pay
off your mortgage balance when you sell. If your
mortgage doesn't have a due-on-sale clause, the buyer
of your house may be able to take over your mortgage
—something that would make your house more sal-
able if interest rates have risen.

With an adjustable-rate mortgage, look for caps
that favor the borrower—infrequent rate raises, and
a low limit on these raises over the years.

Now that you know the basics, it's time to go mortgage shopping in earnest.

## Looking for Mr. Low Down Payment

For first-time buyers, the toughest part of joining
the home-ownership ranks is coming up with a 20
percent down payment on a conventional (nongovern-
mental) loan. The best bet for these buyers is usually
a loan backed by the Veterans Administration or the
Federal Housing Administration.   FHA

The VA guarantees as much as the first $36,000 of
any approved loan, effectively replacing a buyer's
down payment with a government guarantee to the
lender. In fact, it's possible to get a VA-backed loan
with *no* down payment. You'll have to pay a management fee of 1 percent of the loan, but even that can be
rolled into the total amount financed. The one big
catch in qualifying for VA-backed loans: You have to

be a veteran. (But you can assume one even if you're not a veteran.)

The closest thing to a loan with no down payment is an FHA-insured loan. You have to put down only 3 percent on the first $25,000 borrowed, and 5 percent down on anything above that. Income requirements are also slightly more liberal than for other types of loans.

You can't borrow more than $90,000 under the FHA program, unless you live in a high-cost area. In that case, the amount is closer to $101,250. Also plan on paying a fee of up to 3.8 percent of the amount borrowed.

On top of their other advantages, some economists feel the interest rate on FHA- and VA-backed loans is a good deal. "Thirty-year VA-backed loans have been at around 10.5 percent, which is attractive compared with interest rates for much of this decade," says Richard Peach, deputy chief economist with the Mortgage Bankers Association (MBA).

Don't let those old horror stories about red-tape delays on FHA-backed loans discourage you from applying. "The FHA program has been streamlined, and lenders are now much more willing to process those applications," says MBA senior director Brian Chappelle.

Loans subsidized through state lending agencies are another option for first-time buyers. The required down payment is usually less than 10 percent and sometimes under 5 percent.

Don't count on these programs, though; demand for the low-cost loans can quickly overrun supply. For example, when California recently offered loans at 8.6 percent, one lender used up its allocation of funds in three hours.

Finally, you might be able to get a good old-fashioned low down payment loan. "There are still some 95 percent loan-to-value mortgages available, but you have to shop for them," says Sharon Millett, a vice president of McCann Realty in Portland, Maine.

It'll be easier to qualify for a loan with a low down payment if you have good career prospects and don't owe much money. "You'll probably need to have a relatively low ratio of housing cost to total income, as well as very few debts," says Mark Obrinsky, an economist with the U.S. League of Savings Institutions.

## People on the Upward (Income) Track

Adjustable-rate mortgages, which represented nearly 70 percent of the conventional loan market at the end of 1987, have become the loan of choice for folks who expect salary increases in the coming years. The reason is simple. ARMs may carry interest rates of 3 percentage points less than fixed-rate loans. That means significantly lower monthly payments. For example, the monthly payment on a $100,000, 30-year fixed-rate loan at 10.6 percent interest is $880.45. On a comparable ARM at 7.97 percent the monthly payment is $659.16—a hefty $221.29 per month savings.

The drawback of ARMs is that your interest rate and monthly mortgage payment could go higher. (Any ARM you take should have caps restricting rate increases to no more than 2 percentage points in any year and 5 total percentage points over the life of the loan.)

But for many people choosing ARMs, bright financial futures more than balance those risks. "For the young professionals, ARMs have worked out well," Millett says.

One way to lower your interest rate a little more, if you've got some money in the bank, is to pay extra "points." (A point is equal to 1 percent of the loan amount, and lenders typically charge 1 to 3 points on their loans.) Many lenders will quote interest rates varying by the number of points paid.

## Movers, and Shakers, and Movers

The cost of closing on a loan—property valuation, title search, loan origination fees—typically adds 3 to 6 percent to the purchase price of a home. One alternative if you expect to be moving up or out in a few years: a so-called movable mortgage, which can be transferred from one home to another. "It gives people more flexibility in their financing options," says Hector Gallardo, a mortgage consultant with Chase Home Mortgage in Manhattan.

Flexibility isn't free, though. The interest rate on Chase's Home Mortgage movable is about an eighth of a percentage point higher than on its conventional loan. There's also a transfer fee of $500, which is considerably less than the 3 to 6 percent it would cost to obtain an entirely new mortgage.

What if you're buying up, and the balance of your old mortgage doesn't cover the cost of your new home? You can get an add-on mortgage from Chase, but you'll pay an origination fee and closing costs on the add-on amount.

"This is a good bet for someone who anticipates being transferred by his or her employer within a few years," says Ray Stringer, vice president with the Harris-Engelhard Group, a mortgage-rate survey company.

Pretty sure you'll be in a home for only a few years, but can't find an institution offering a movable mortgage? Then get an ARM that doesn't change for three years or longer. Your payments will be lower than with a fixed-rate loan, but the long span between origination and adjustment of the interest rate on the

ARM will give you, in effect, a fixed-rate short-term loan. Recently, at Bell Federal Savings in Chicago, you could get a 9.75 percent mortgage that would be adjusted only after five years.

"There's no question that people who know they're going to move in four or five years should consider the most aggressively priced ARM they can find. They'll probably be gone before anything bad can happen," says Richard Rosenthal, head of a real estate agency in Los Angeles that bears his name. "On the other hand, it's certainly not something I'd recommend for a retired couple or anyone else who'd be worried about long-term interest rate shifts."

## Equity-Lovers

One frustration for people who think of their monthly mortgage payment as an investment is seeing how little principal is paid off in the early years of a 30-year mortgage. And with lower tax rates, knowing that more than 95 percent of your monthly payment is tax-deductible interest isn't even the consolation it used to be.

But you can own your home in 15 to 19 years instead of 30 with loans that build up your equity much faster.

Your monthly payments will be about 15 to 20 percent higher, but the total interest paid on the loan will be cut by about 40 to 55 percent.

There are three basic options for people looking to pay off their home loan quickly:

1. *Fifteen-year loans.* Payable monthly, they're usually available at one-fourth to one-half of a percentage point less than 30-year loans.
2. *Biweekly loans.* You make half of a 30-year monthly loan payment every 14 days. The 26

payments equal 13 monthly payments a year instead of 12, and cut the term of your loan to about 18.5 years.

Many institutions offering biweeklies electronically debit an account you have with the lender to minimize paperwork costs. So be sure not to let the balance in such an account fall. "The lender may impose huge penalties on a biweekly mortgage if the money is not in your account," says Forrest Pafenberg, director of real estate finance research with the National Association of Realtors. "Obviously, you shouldn't take this kind of mortgage loan if you don't have a healthy cash flow."

3. *Personalized prepayment plans.* If you like the 15-year concept and don't mind a little extra bookkeeping, simply take a 30-year fixed-rate mortgage and make extra payments of principal monthly. Check to be sure that you won't have to deal with prepayment penalties if you pursue this tactic, and be certain that your lender knows that the extra money is to be applied against your outstanding loan balance.

## People without Documentation (or Time)

A lender might ask you for any of the following before approving a standard home loan: W-2 statements, payroll stubs, income-tax forms, bank statements, proof of employment, 1099 forms—you get the idea. Woe to anyone in a hurry to close, or who recently started a business and doesn't have some of this evidence.

No problem. For 25 to 30 percent down, you can get a loan under a program like GMAC Mortgage Quick-Loan, available in most states. No employment verification, no income verification, no tax forms required.

Just a standard credit check. "This type of loan is ideal for self-employed borrowers who have a difficult time demonstrating their borrowing and income ability by traditional means," says Mike McFall of GMAC.

## The Unsure

Okay, so you can afford to make a hefty down payment and your income flow is reliable. But you're one of those people who knows it won't rain—unless you leave home without your umbrella. You're afraid that if you take out an ARM, interest rates will skyrocket and you'll wish you had a fixed-rate loan. If you go for a fixed rate, interest rates will plummet and you'll have to pay to refinance.

Well, guess what? You can get a fixed-rate mortgage that converts to an ARM ... or an ARM that converts to a fixed rate. Many lenders charge slightly higher interest rates on these than on nonconvertibles and assess fees ranging from $200 to 1 percent of the loan value. Some convertibles have no transfer fees, but that may be offset by higher interest rates, so shop around and compare. Conversion typically must be done within the first five years of the loan.

Don't even *try* collecting all the variations on this basic theme. Shearson Lehman Mortgage's fixed-rate loan can be converted to a lower fixed rate for $100 plus 0.25 percent of the loan balance. GMAC has a fixed rate that automatically converts to an ARM in the sixth year, and may then be converted back to a fixed rate before the end of the eighth year for $250. The permutations are seemingly limited only by the creativity of marketers.

One other variation worth noting is the fixed-payment ARM marketed by Mortgage Refinance in Boston. It's a loan with an expected term of 15 years, with the length of the loan (instead of your monthly payment) changing if interest rates go up or down. In a worst-case scenario, with interest rates hitting their annual and life-of-loan caps as quickly as possible, the loan term would be about 25 years.

No matter what your situation may be, don't just go with whatever the first lender you see puts in front of you. With more than 150 ARM programs in the field, each with its own terms and disclosures, you have a wide choice.

Marilyn Quinn and Jim Siedlecki of Wheaton, Maryland, wanted to build up equity in their first home as fast as possible. Their solution: a 15-year VA-backed loan.

Recently the couple paid $62,000 for their duplex, financing it with a 12 percent loan. "We got a lower interest rate than if we'd taken a 30-year loan, so the difference in monthly payments wasn't that great," says Quinn, a research assistant for a defense consulting firm. "Plus, a 15-year loan just didn't sound as scary as a 30-year loan."

"We figured that this is a major investment for us —our only investment, really," says Siedlecki, who works for the Bureau of the Census. "I don't like the idea of a long-term loan with so little [equity] to show for it. So, when we found we had the option of paying it off twice as fast, we took it."

Being able to buy a home with minimal cash up front, thanks to Jim's prior military service, also took care of some financial hobgoblins. And when interest rates plummeted in 1986, the couple exorcised part of their financial burden by refinancing their loan at 9.5 percent. That cut their monthly mortgage payment from $803.72 to $732.62.

"I just didn't want to put a lot of money down, and I didn't want to worry about my monthly payments changing," remembers Rebecca Moreo of Seattle, who bought a one-bedroom condominium for $57,500 recently.

Moreo, 26, had to put only about $2,100 down on her condo, which is financed by an FHA-backed loan at 10.5 percent. She paid 1 point on the loan. "I could have gotten it for about 10 percent, but that would have meant paying an extra point or two, and I wanted to keep my up-front costs low," says Moreo, a marketing representative with IBM.

She would seem the perfect candidate for an ARM —young, single, and with good career potential—but opted for the safety of a fixed rate instead. The reason: Part of her salary comes from commissions, and that creates enough financial uncertainty without her worrying about interest rate spikes. Her monthly payment is $584, plus $47 in condo fees.

FHA-backed loans are assumable, and that also fits in nicely with Moreo's plans. She figures on staying in the condo for only three to five years, and knows an assumable loan will make her property more attractive to buyers if interest rates increase.

Alternatively, she may keep the condo as an investment after she moves. "I'm in a good rental area, and who wouldn't like to be able to see the Space Needle from their balcony?"

Patrick and Linda Moore's new house is the proverbial dream—a four-bedroom, custom-built home 65 miles north of New York City. Patrick found that the dream mortgage on the property was an ARM at 7.5 percent, with caps of 2 percentage points annually and 6 percentage points over the life of the loan. "I ran the numbers through an accounting package on my home computer and found that, in the worst case, the ARM would cost us more than the fixed-rate loans only after 10 years," says Patrick.

The cost of dreams for Patrick, a commercial-property insurance salesman, and Linda, a part-time music instructor, was $194,500. The couple rolled the proceeds from the sale of their previous house into the new property, leaving them with a $115,000 mortgage. Their monthly payments, including taxes, are about $1,050—a couple of hundred dollars less, Patrick figures, than if they'd taken a fixed-rate mortgage. "I'd rather have the low payments and use the extra money for all the other things you need when you move into a new home," he says.

The couple, who have two children, comparison-shopped through their local newspaper, which publishes interest rates on standard mortgages offered by area lenders. "The most our payments would increase in any one year is about $150 a month," Patrick says. "I can live with that."

## Saving for a Down Payment
## Regular Savings

Planning on savings to make that big down payment? Here's how your interest adds up when you make regular monthly deposits to your savings account. Figure the interest rate on your account and how much you can afford to save each month. Then follow the chart across to see how long it will take you to meet your savings goals.

| Interest Rate | Monthly Deposits | After 1 Year | 3 Years | 5 Years |
|---|---|---|---|---|
| 6% | $ 50 | $ 620.28 | $ 1,979.97 | $ 3,515.56 |
|  | 100 | 1,240.55 | 3,959.94 | 7,031.13 |
|  | 500 | 6,202.75 | 19,799.70 | 35,155.63 |
| 8% | 50 | 627.23 | 2,045.12 | 3,712.71 |
|  | 100 | 1,254.45 | 4,090.25 | 7,425.43 |
|  | 500 | 6,272.27 | 20,451.24 | 37,127.14 |
| 10% | 50 | 634.28 | 2,113.07 | 3,924.24 |
|  | 100 | 1,268.55 | 4,226.13 | 7,848.48 |
|  | 500 | 6,342.77 | 21,130.67 | 39,242.39 |

## Lump-Sum Savings

A bonus, an inheritance, or a large tax refund can give
you a head start for your down payment. Here's how
your interest adds up at various rates:

| Interest Rate | Monthly Deposits | After 1 Year | 3 Years | 5 Years |
|---|---|---|---|---|
| 6% | $ 5,000 | $ 5,313.58 | $ 6,000.98 | $ 6,777.30 |
|  | 10,000 | 10,627.16 | 12,001.96 | 13,554.61 |
|  | 15,000 | 15,940.75 | 18,002.94 | 20,331.91 |
| 8% | 5,000 | 5,422.41 | 6,377.30 | 7,500.34 |
|  | 10,000 | 10,844.82 | 12,754.59 | 15,000.68 |
|  | 15,000 | 16,267.22 | 19,131.89 | 22,501.02 |
|  | 20,000 | 21,689.63 | 25,509.18 | 30,001.36 |
| 10% | 5,000 | 5,533.46 | 6,777.19 | 8,300.47 |
|  | 10,000 | 11,066.91 | 13,554.38 | 16,600.94 |
|  | 15,000 | 16,600.37 | 20,331.57 | 24,901.41 |
|  | 20,000 | 22,133.83 | 27,108.75 | 33,201.87 |

Interest is compounded daily in these charts. Payment
of federal, state, and local taxes on savings is not cal-
culated.

## The Average Mortgage Payment

In 1987, the average American home owner paid $935 a month, $11,220 a year, toward a fixed-rate mortgage. That person's gross monthly income was $3,388, or $40,652 a year. Over the years, as the table below shows, a fixed-rate mortgage may cost more than an adjustable-rate mortgage—or more, or the same.

### Percentage of Pretax Income That Goes Toward a Mortgage

| Year | Fixed-Rate Mortgage | Adjustable-Rate Mortgage |
|------|---------------------|--------------------------|
| 1983 | 31.1% | 28.9% |
| 1984 | 28.9 | 28.1 |
| 1985 | 28.9 | 27.7 |
| 1986 | 27.9 | 28.2 |
| 1987 | 27.6 | 28.3 |

Source: U.S. Housing Markets.

## Comparing Mortgage Offers

If you're going mortgage hunting, use this worksheet to compare offers. Try to avoid points (loan charges, each equal to 1 percent of the mortgage), loan fees, prepayment penalties, and acceleration clauses. Try to earn interest on the home insurance and property taxes that the lender may collect from you—"escrow with interest."

| Lender | 1 | 2 | 3 |
|---|---|---|---|
| Name, phone | | | |
| Loan amount | | | |
| Down payment | | | |
| Term | | | |
| Interest rate | | | |
| Interest type (fixed, ARM, etc.) | | | |
|   Frequency of rate changes | | | |
|   Limit on single changes | | | |
|   Limit on total changes | | | |
|   Interest-rate index | | | |
| Points | | | |
| Loan fees | | | |
| Mortgage insurance? | | | |
| Prepayment penalty? | | | |
| Acceleration clause? | | | |
| Escrow with interest? | | | |

# A Concise Guide to Mortgages

This list of mortgages and the commentary were prepared by the Federal Trade Commission.

| Type | Description |
|---|---|
| Fixed-rate mortgage | Fixed interest rate, usually long-term; equal monthly payments of principal and interest until debt is paid in full. |
| Adjustable-rate mortgage | Interest rate changes are based on a financial index, resulting in possible changes in your monthly payments, loan term, and/or principal. Some plans have rate or payment caps. |
| Renegotiable-rate mortgage (rollover) | Interest rate and monthly payments are constant for several years; changes possible thereafter. Long-term mortgage. |
| Balloon mortgage | Monthly payments based on fixed interest rate; usually short-term; payments may cover interest only with principal due in full at term end. |
| Graduated-payment mortgage | Lower monthly payments rise gradually (usually over 5–10 years), then level off for duration of term. With adjustable interest rate, additional payment changes possible if index changes. |
| Shared-appreciation mortgage | Below-market interest rate and lower monthly payments, in exchange for a share of profits when property is sold or on a specified date. Many variations. |
| Assumable mortgage | Buyer takes over seller's original, below-market-rate mortgage. |
| Seller take-back | Seller provides all or part of financing with a first or second mortgage. |

# A Concise Guide to Mortgages

### Considerations

Offers stability and long-term tax advantages. Interest rates may be higher than with other types of financing. New fixed rates are rarely assumable.

Readily available. Starting interest rate is slightly below market, but payments can increase sharply and frequently if index increases. Payment caps prevent wide fluctuations in payments but may cause negative amortization (your debt actually increases). Rate caps limit amount total debt can expand.

Less frequent changes in interest rate offer some stability.

Offers low monthly payments but possibly no equity until loan is fully paid. When due, loan must be paid off or refinanced. Refinancing poses high risk if rates climb.

Easier to qualify for. Buyer's income must be able to keep pace with scheduled payment increases. With an adjustable rate, payment increases beyond the graduated payments can result in additional negative amortization.

If home appreciates greatly, total cost of loan jumps. If home fails to appreciate, projected increase in value may still be due, requiring refinancing at possibly higher rates.

Lowers monthly payments. May be prohibited if due-on-sale clause is in original mortgage. Not permitted on most new fixed-rate mortgages.

May offer a below-market interest rate; may have a balloon payment requiring full payment in a few years or refinancing at market rates, which could increase debt sharply.

# A Concise Guide to Mortgages

| Type | Description |
| --- | --- |
| Wraparound | Seller keeps original low-rate mortgage. Buyer makes payments to seller, who forwards a portion to the lender holding original mortgage. Offers lower effective interest rate on total transaction. |
| Growing equity mortgage (rapid payoff mortgage) | Fixed interest rate but monthly payments may vary according to agreed-upon schedule or index. |
| Land contract | Seller retains original mortgage. No transfer of title until loan is fully paid. Equal monthly payments based on below-market interest rate with unpaid principal due at loan end. |
| Buy-down | Developer (or third party) provides an interest subsidy that lowers monthly payments during the first few years of the loan. Can have fixed or adjustable interest rate. |
| Rent with option | Renter pays "option fee" for right to purchase property at specified time and agreed-upon price. Rent may or may not be applied to sale price. |
| Reverse annuity mortgage (equity conversion) | Borrower owns mortgage-free property and is in need of income. Lender makes monthly payments to borrower, using property as collateral. |
| Zero-rate and low-rate mortgage | Appears to be completely or almost interest free. Large down payment and one-time finance charge, then loan is repaid in fixed monthly payments over short term. |

# A Concise Guide to Mortgages

### Considerations

Lender may call in old mortgage and require higher rate. If buyer defaults, seller must take legal action to collect debt.

Permits rapid payoff of debt because payment increases reduce principal. Buyer's income must be able to keep up with payment increases.

May offer no equity until loan is fully paid. Buyer has few protections if conflict arises during loan.

Offers a break from higher payments during early years. Enables buyer with lower income to qualify. With adjustable-rate mortgage, payments may jump substantially at end of subsidy. Developer may increase selling price.

Enables renter to buy time to obtain down payment and decide whether to purchase. Locks in price during inflationary times. Failure to take option means loss of option fee and rental payments.

Can provide home owners with needed cash. At end of term, borrower must have money available to avoid selling property or refinancing.

Permits quick ownership. May not lower total cost (because of possibly increased sale price). Doesn't offer long-term tax deductions.

# Chapter 7

# Whose Side Is "Your" Agent On?

If you had gone house-hunting some years ago, the agent who drove you around might not have warned you that, to reach one house after a rainstorm, you would need a rowboat. Or that the owner of another house for sale had just died of AIDS. Or that still another house on the market had been the scene of a horrible mass-murder.

In fact, the agent—who was probably as warm and friendly as Dale Carnegie himself—may not have revealed to you that he or she was in the pocket of the home owner. Though the agent may never have met or even spoken to the home owner, *the agent was legally bound to meet the seller's full asking price, on terms totally favorable to the seller.*

So, if you had confided to the agent, "I'll offer $80,000, but go as high as $83," the agent would have been obliged to advise the seller, "Hold out for $83,000."

In fact, the agent might not have passed along to you such sensible advice as that, in any written offer, you stipulate that your purchase is "subject to a satisfactory report from a house inspector and a termite inspector."

* * *

Today, fortunately, the winds of change are blowing fresh air into the real estate field. Worried about lawsuits, the powerful National Association of Realtors has urged the states to require that agents use disclosure forms to inform buyers that they work for the sellers. Approximately a dozen states have already enacted such legislation or are planning to do so shortly. Nine states have disclosure rules that are already in effect: California, Colorado, Hawaii, Indiana, Minnesota, Oregon, Utah, Washington, and Wisconsin.

Meanwhile, more and more courts have been throwing the book at agents who didn't warn buyers about important flaws in houses they went on to purchase, especially if the flaws weren't readily visible—termite infestation, for instance. Reason: Although agents must be loyal to sellers, they also must be fair and honest with buyers.

A few courts have recently put the fear of God into agents by holding them liable for innocently passing along misinformation—for example, that a water well on the property would be adequate for the buyer's family.

 Other courts have insisted that agents make a "reasonably competent and diligent inspection" of residential property to uncover any defects—for example, that the house was built on shaky soil and might be subject to a landslide. (In this case, it was.)

Still, although agents may be far more fair in dealing with buyers these days, remain on your guard if you're shopping for a house. Here's what you can do to keep from becoming a homing pigeon.

You're usually better off playing the field rather than dealing with just one agent. Agents tend to push properties listed with their firm, paying far less attention to those available via a multiple-listing service (where brokers pool their properties for sale).

If you do want only one agent, choose a veteran, not someone who just entered the field. Look for advanced credentials, such as Graduate of the Realtor Institute, Certified Residential Specialist, Realtor, or Realtor Associate. And aim for someone who tells you, right off the bat, "I'll try to be fair with you, but I work for the sellers."

*Never* confide your negotiating strategy to an agent. *Never* reveal that you must buy a house posthaste (because, for example, your apartment lease is coming due). *Never* confess that you've fallen in love with a particular house. *Never* reveal how high you may go in bidding for a house.

Even if the agent doesn't suggest it, don't sign anything without the advice of a lawyer. Second-best: Write on the document, "Subject to the approval of my lawyer."

Any offer you make should be also subject to a satisfactory report from a house inspector. (See Chapter 9.)

Finally, beware of agents who:

- Show you a shack, a hovel, a "handyman's special," and finally a halfway decent house—which, by comparison, will look like a royal mansion. The agent has been setting you up.
- Show you houses for $90,000 and up—after you have carefully explained that you can afford only $80,000 houses. (Agents tell themselves, "All buyers are liars.")
- Show you houses only at night—so you may not notice imperfections that would be apparent during the day. (Like water stains on the dining room ceiling, from the bathroom above.)
- Twist your arm to make an immediate offer be-

cause someone else is supposedly about to pounce on the house. (One lawyer says that if you can believe agents, the entire Red Chinese army is about to buy the house you're considering.)

- Brush off any valid objections you raise about a house. Sample dialogue from a guidebook for agents:

  *Buyer:* There's no dining room.
  *Agent:* One less room to clean.

- Show you two or three houses, then act thunderstruck and outraged that you haven't made a choice.

  Consider the case of Charles and Diane Thompson of Novato, California. When they searched for another home in Novato, they spent six months and examined 189 homes before making a decision. Needless to say, they are well satisfied with their choice. The agent they used, Warren Edgar, says, "I didn't mind. They're great people, and I knew they'd buy eventually."

Another course you can take to protect your interests is to hire your own agent. Choose someone you respect, someone familiar with the area, someone who can negotiate skillfully. About a thousand agents have had special training as "buyer's brokers," though you can ask any agent at all to represent you.

You can pay your agent by the hour ($45 to $95), a flat fee ($1,000 to $5,000), or a percentage of the sales price (1.5 to 4 percent). Says William R. Broadbent, a buyer's broker in Obispo, California, "A buyer's broker can often negotiate a price down and save you an amount equal to or greater than his fee."

Your own agent can bargain over other terms, too. You may want the settlement date delayed until you have sold your own house (if you're not a first-time buyer), or the sale made contingent upon your getting a mortgage at a minimum interest rate.

Your own agent can also level with you about which parts of town are the most desirable, which have the best schools, and which neighborhoods are subject to flooding.

Finally, your own agent can show you more houses for sale than seller's agents can. A buyer's agent can negotiate with people selling their own houses, invoking the magic words, "No commission." Your agent may even persuade home owners whose houses aren't for sale that they *should* be.

When Millie Munding, a retired sheriff's detective in Bakersfield, California, decided to move to Ventura, she decided to hire a buyer's broker. "I wanted someone working for *me*," she says. She hired George Rosenberg, who compiles the *Buyer's Brokers Registry* (available for $25 plus $2.40 for postage from P.O. Box 23275, Ventura, CA 93002). Rosenberg drove her around, and she was captivated by several duplexes she spotted; for extra income, she could rent out one floor. Rosenberg wrote to the owners. Several were interested in selling, and Munding wound up buying one. "I got an excellent price," she says.

A buyer may even end up not paying an agent a penny.

Sellers typically pay agents a 5 or 7 percent commission. Usually half goes to the "listing" agent, whose broker originally signed up the seller. Half goes to the "selling" agent, who learns about the house through the local multiple-listing service and finds a genuine buyer.

Your own agent could tell the home-owner's agent, "Look, there's no selling agent here. Why not pay *me* the 3 percent you would otherwise pay a selling agent?" If that happens, you wind up not spending a cent.

But there can be a problem. A buyer's agent paid by

the seller might be considered the *seller's* agent, too—
and thus be guilty of what lawyers call "undisclosed
dual agency." If the buyer and seller wind up in court,
says Roger D. Butters, associate counsel of the National Association of Realtors, the agent could be "behind the eight-ball."

A buyer's agent could also get into hot water by
helping the buyer purchase a house that the agent
had already been trying to peddle. In such a case, it
would help if buyer and seller have agreed, in writing,
to have one agent representing both of them.

Still, buyers' brokers may become more common.
One company, Buyer One in Chandler, Arizona, is
even planning to open up offices around the country.
One of its advertisements states:

WE WORK ONLY FOR BUYERS. And that's
what makes us unique. In fact, Buyer One is the
ONLY major real estate company that works exclu-
sively for buyers.

Why is that important? You may not be aware of
it, but most real estate agents owe their loyalty to
the seller, not the buyer, whether the home you
choose is listed by their company or not.

But we're different. Our loyalty is to buyers.
Only buyers. . . .

NO LISTINGS. EVER. We do not take listings. If
we did, we would owe our loyalty to the seller. And
then we would be just like other real estate companies, who make twice as much if they can sell you
their own listing.

We have nothing to sell except service. So you'll
never feel pressure from us to buy one home over
another. We'll help you find the home you want to
own. But our real job is to use our expertise to get
you the best deal.

OUR AGENTS MAKE THE SAME NO MATTER WHAT YOU SPEND. We work for you. So we pay our agents the same amount whether your home costs $50,000 or $500,000. Which means that they have no reason to push you toward a more expensive home. Other agents make more when you spend more....

Most people spend four months searching for the right home. But it usually takes our clients just two weeks—often less. Because they don't have to spend weeks driving all over the place looking at homes that aren't even close to what they want....

OUR SERVICES DON'T COST YOU A CENT. Virtually every home on the market, new or resale, has a commission built into its price. The money our company earns comes from that commission, which the seller will pay whether you use our services or not. But remember—if you don't use us, you probably won't be represented.

If you ever believe that an agent hasn't been fair with you, complain—first to the agent and to the agent's broker, then to your state's real estate licensing board and to your local Board of Realtors. A complaint may do the trick. The buyer of the house whose owner had died of AIDS got the estate to pay for disinfecting the house.

If you think of suing, your logical target should be the agent, not the seller, who may be off for parts unknown. Also, Robert S. Treece, a Denver lawyer who specializes in professional malpractice, notes that courts may regard a seller as well as a buyer as mere babes in the woods. But they expect agents to be full-fledged experts.

Buyers have obtained damages and even canceled sales when sellers and their agents didn't reveal that:

- A house someone had purchased had just been condemned by the Board of Health.
- Improvements—such as a second floor—had been added in violation of the zoning or building code.
- A house was in an area officially designated as a flood zone.
- A house was infested with insects—and it had been shown only in the daytime, with all the lights blazing, to discourage these other tenants from putting in an appearance.

Don't despair if the contract you signed contained an "as is" clause: You accepted the house in its present condition. An "as is" clause doesn't mean much if the house had flaws you could not have noticed, but the seller must have known about. A buyer can be expected to observe that a stairway is falling down, one court has held, but not "a subterranean creek in the backyard or an unexploded bomb buried in the basement."

Don't give up hope even if, while checking out a house, you somehow overlooked an important defect.

In Illinois, a man noticed a pool of water in the basement of a house he was inspecting. When he inquired whether there was a flooding problem, the owner replied that the water was caused by a leaking valve on the sump pumps. The man bought the property.

After the closing, the basement continued to flood, so he brought suit. The seller and his agents argued that the buyer certainly knew that the basement leaked. But a court held that the buyer didn't know how *bad* the problem was. Evidence showed that when the house was built, its foundation was lower than the groundwater level—a flaw that made the house worth $22,500 less (according to appraisers) than the sales price. And the seller must have known how serious the leakage was: During "several preclosing inspections," the judge noted, "there were two or more sump pumps in the basement, which ran almost continually."

In the future, expect more and more suits against real estate agents. Predictions are that they will be held accountable for selling houses near toxic waste areas as well as houses with radon contamination.

### Bargains in Brokers

Whether you're buying or selling a house, you can save hundreds of dollars by using a discount broker, or by using a regular broker and persuading him or her to lower the commission.

"People mistakenly assume that brokers' commissions are set by law when they're not," says Glenn Crelin, vice president of research for the National Association of Realtors. "They're always negotiable."

Buyer's Choice, a Florida franchise firm, offers all the services of a regular broker except one: showing the houses. This cuts down on salaries. You pay a flat fee of $875 at the closing, reports Sharon James, the firm's president. On a $70,000 home, the seller saves about $4,000 in commissions. Buyer's Choice provides the seller with FOR SALE signs and advertising help; the buyer gets a computerized list of properties for sale, and arranges with sellers to see their homes.

Another discount broker, First Federal Realty Monaco, in Smithtown, New York, charges a flat fee of $5,990. The firm deals in houses over $200,000, and its members do show houses to prospective buyers.

Look for other discount brokers in the Yellow Pages of your local phone book, or by reading a newspaper's real estate listings.

# Chapter 8

# Haggling Over the Price

To quote a famous anthropologist, "Americans tend to look down upon people who haggle." But unless you're willing to bargain, you may pay far too much for any big-ticket item—particularly houses, whose prices usually have some elasticity built into them.

Before you offer a bid on any house you're interested in, do some research. Is it high-priced for the area? How long has it been on the market? Why are the owners moving? Is the local market itself slow or active? If the owners have been trying to sell for six months, and they have already bought a new house 700 miles away, you may be in the catbird seat.

Decide what you would love to pay for a house—and decide the highest amount you'll be willing to spring for.

Here are rules that professional negotiators follow:

- Be careful not to antagonize the sellers. Don't criticize their taste in furnishings, or express your annoyance at their stubbornness in refusing to lower the price. Some sellers have become so angry at buyers that they've refused to sell to them at any price.

- Start with a low bid—to dampen the sellers' expectations. But don't make your first bid so outlandish that they slam the door on you. A bid 15 percent below the asking price may be appropriate—for example, offering $68,000 for a house priced at $80,000. (Sellers usually pad their prices by 5 to 10 percent.)
- Try to get a concession for every concession you make. After you bid (say) $68,000, wait for the sellers to come down a bit—say, to $77,000.
- Make your concessions smaller and smaller. If you want the house for $74,000, your bids might go from $68,000 to $71,000 to $72,500 to $73,000. Your concessions have gone up $3,000, $1,500, and $500. That suggests that you're reaching the limit of your budget.
- Ignore any seemingly final statements that the sellers make, such as "That's my final offer" or "Take it or leave it." Just keep negotiating.
- If the sellers says, "Let's split the difference," and that would be more than $74,000, reply, "I'd like to, but I can't afford it."
- If the sellers refuse to budge, you might take the risk of waiting them out. It depends on how badly you want the house.
- Offer other concessions besides money for the house. Suggest moving up the closing date, for example. Or paying extra for the lawn equipment if the sellers will leave it.
- Be imaginative. In 1947, a pharmaceutical tycoon wanted to sell his Virginia estate for $275,000. A buyer came forward—but insisted on paying $25,000 extra for a Gilbert Stuart painting of George Washington that hung in the foyer. The seller refused to part with it. Their agent suggested that they toss a coin. They agreed; the buyer won; the house was sold.

- Finally, if the house is reasonably priced, in a desirable area, and a "creampuff" (as agents call a spiffy place), don't bargain too hard. Your first priority is to own the house—not to win at the bargaining table.

# Chapter 9

# Dealing with
# a Home Inspector

Julie and Ray Leiter finally found what seemed the perfect home—until they received the inspection report they had ordered. The house's foundation was beginning to buckle, and the buttressing needed was likely to cost over $10,000. Also, the discoloration of the living-room ceiling turned out to be due to a moisture problem: The bathroom above had not been adequately ventilated.

Disappointed, the Leiters took advantage of a clause in their sales contract allowing them to bow out if the inspection report uncovered serious defects. "We figured that if we were going to spend that much for repairs, we'd rather pay more up front for another house and not have all that work," Julie says.

The Leiters soon found another house they liked, in Flemington, New Jersey. The inspector's report indicated that the place needed a new roof—no minor item. The seller reduced the price by $6,000. Sale consummated.

Ordering an inspection report on any residence you're interested in buying is, of course, essential. HouseMaster of America, the country's largest house-inspection service, estimates that two out of five houses offered for sale have at least one serious defect —one costing at least $500 to repair or replace.

The question is: Once you have an inspection report, what do you do with it?

## What the Contract Should Say

You can spare yourself grief later on if, before the inspection, you and the seller agree on what to do about serious defects.

In some areas, like New York City, inspections are usually conducted before any papers are signed. Seller and buyer can haggle over the cost of any repairs before a legally binding document is brought out.

In other areas, inspections are conducted after contracts are signed, but the contracts themselves make provision for the inspections. Ken Austin, president of HouseMaster, reports that a typical contract will state: "Sale is contingent upon an inspection report's indicating that no repair or replacement above $500 [typically] is called for. If such is not the case, the owner has the right to (a) repair or replace the defect; (b) negotiate the problem with the buyer; or (c) withdraw the offer. The buyer can withdraw unless the owner chooses (a) or (b)."

In short, unless the owner and buyer come to terms about expensive repairs, all bets are off.

## Causes for Alarm

Suppose you've just received a report about a house you're interested in. The report probably provides a summary page, pointing out immediate areas of concern, or those likely to be costly to repair or replace. These problems may also be red-flagged in the text.

When you read the report itself, look for alarming

words—like "poor," "significant," "excessive," and "substantial." (Example: "Condition of driveway is poor.") Check the life expectancies the report provides for major mechanical systems. And look for ballpark estimates of the cost of work that needs to be done, although in the case of severe structural damage, inspectors may decline even to venture guesstimates.

The most serious problems, according to HouseMaster, are:

- *Structural defects.* Resupporting a wall, for example, can cost $3,000 or more.
- *Roofing.* Asphalt shingling can cost $1,800 to $2,500; wood shingling, $3,500.
- *Heating and cooling.* A new warm-air furnace can cost $1,500 to $2,000; a new water boiler, $2,000 to $2,500; and a new air-conditioning compressor, $750 to $1,000.
- *Plumbing.* Replumbing an entire house can cost thousands; a new shower pan (the basin beneath the tile), $900 to $1,600.
- *Electricity.* Upgrading a panel can cost $600 to $1,000; rewiring a house can cost thousands.
- *Residing.* The range of prices runs from $8,000 to 20,000, depending on the house's size and the materials used.

House inspectors may or may not be authorized to conduct termite or radon inspections, depending on state laws.

With condominiums and cooperatives, inspectors typically emphasize the interiors. But they should also check the common elements; buyers may be forced to share in the cost of replacing a furnace, for example. And new houses should be inspected, too— before any warranty expires. Austin reports that although new houses tend to need fewer repairs, they're typically not constructed as well as existing houses. "Houses built prior to 1950 were built better," he says. "Most of the good craftsmen are gone."

## Dealing with Problems

Let's say that the inspection report indicates that the roof of the house you're interested in needs replacing. Should the seller pay? Should you? Should you split the cost?

Generally, agree to split it. Sure, you didn't count on buying a house with a rotten roof. But you didn't expect a brand-new roof, either. So sharing is fair.

Alas, some sellers will be stubborn, and refuse to help pay part of the cost of any repairs, put money into an escrow account, or lower the price.

When Julie Leiter told the seller of that house (mentioned earlier) that the foundation needed buttressing, he grumpily replied, "It's been standing for 17 years, it'll stand for 17 more years."

Your response will depend on whether you feel the house is undervalued or fairly valued. (If you felt it was *over*valued, you probably wouldn't be interested in the first place.) If you're getting a bargain, and you're crazy about the place, you might agree to absorb the cost yourself. But try to persuade the seller to give you a break in some other area—such as by giving you the lawn equipment, or moving up (or back) the move-in date.

If (a) the house if fairly valued; (b) the repair or replacement is costly; and (c) the seller won't lower the price or help defray the cost of repairs, try to bargain. If the housing market in the area is sluggish, and you know the owner has been trying to unload the place for months because he or she has bought another house across the country, you might hang tough. A lot depends on how much you want the place. The rule, says Austin, is "Whoever wants it most pays the most."

Some other rules:

1. Don't nickel-and-dime the seller. If you have a good price on a house you like, don't risk losing the sale because of relatively small amounts—the cost of replacing a small cracked window, for example. Says Ronald Passaro of Res-I-Tec, an inspection service in Bethel, Connecticut, "If you're not buying a brand-new house, you've got to expect replacements and repairs."

   Some sellers make bargaining into a contest; don't be afraid of "losing" if you will wind up with a good house at a good price. "If everything suits you otherwise," suggests Austin, "bend a little."

2. If you and the seller are at an impasse, suggest that the real estate agent cut his or her commission, to help cover the cost of repairs. Most agents prefer a smaller profit to no profit at all.

3. Consider walking away from a deal where the defects are outside the house. Passaro, who founded the American Society of Home Inspectors, believes that almost all serious problems can be corrected—but is wary about houses built on a swamp, for example. "There may be structural problems there, with houses leaning or even falling down," he says. "Even that can be corrected, but it would scare me. Problems inside or directly underneath a house I can deal with, but I don't know about something happening 200 to 300 feet beneath the ground."

4. Don't let the seller handle the repairs without your input. He or she may just patch a roof that needs replacing, or use the cheapest carpenter/electrician/mason, who in turn uses the cheapest

materials. Insist that any repairs or replacements be done by someone you approve of, who uses materials you accept. Your home inspector can give you impartial guidance.

---

### Hiring a House Inspector

To obtain names, contact the American Society of Home Inspectors, 3299 K St. N.W., Washington, DC 20007 (202-842-3906). The society will also send you free literature.

Or ask your lawyer or lending institution for recommendations. But check that those recommended have passed the educational and professional requirements to belong to the society.

Give preference to any inspector who will provide a warranty on the report's findings.

Expect to pay $100 to $250, depending on the size of the house, the offering price, and the area of the country.

# Chapter 10

# Who Should Own
the Place?

Whose name goes on the title is no trifling detail.

In taking title you are entering a legal relationship with your co-owner that describes and circumscribes your rights as home owners. This relationship has binding terms that affect you financially and emotionally—now and later. Think through your decision, together with your spouse and your lawyer.

Compare the options: joint or single-party ownership. Try them on and see which fits your needs better. What follows are the broad outlines. There are as many variations as there are individual home buyers.

## Joint Ownership

Many home buyers opt for joint ownership because putting two names on the title is a powerful, enduring symbol of shared monetary and emotional interests in the house. And with several forms to choose from, joint ownership is flexible enough to encompass unusual relationships.

As *tenants in common*—whether you are spouses, friends, relatives, or business associates—you have an undivided, usually equal interest in the house (but the split can vary).

- Each tenant can freely transfer his or her share of the home by sale or will. If no valid will exists for someone who has died, the property will be disposed of in accordance with the state laws.
- If you are husband and wife, no federal gift or estate taxes will be levied if ownership passes, but depending on the value of your estate, you may pay state taxes.
- As unmarried tenants, only that percentage of the home's value owned by the deceased tenant will be taxed (at federal and state levels) upon transfer.
- If one tenant dies, the heir(s) can realize certain federal capital-gains tax advantages if the home is sold. A real estate or estate-planning lawyer can explain these to you.
- Creditors of either tenant can force a sale of your home to free assets to meet the claims (if the equity in your home exceeds your state's homestead exemption).

*Joint tenancy* is similar to tenancy in common except that:

- In the event of one owner's death, the house passes automatically to the surviving tenant— the house's disposition is not covered under a will and therefore escapes probate (often a tedious and costly procedure).
- Joint tenancy is terminated when either tenant sells his or her share of interest in the house to a third party. This action converts the joint tenancy to a tenancy in common between the remaining original tenant and the third party.

*Tenancy by the entirety* is similar to joint tenancy except that:

- It is available only to spouses.
- Spouses share ownership of the house equally— no other splits are possible.
- The right of survivorship can be severed by divorce or mutual agreement only.
- Your home is generally safe from potential creditors (other than the federal government for income taxes) unless you've intentionally chosen this form of ownership to defraud them.
- Many states do not recognize this form of ownership. In those that do, spouses taking title jointly are automatically considered tenants by the entirety, unless another ownership preference is clearly expressed on the title.

*Note:* Approximately 20 states have a community property law that affects joint-ownership arrangements between spouses. If you live in such a state, explore the ramifications with your lawyer.

## Single-Party Ownership

Single-party ownership differs from joint ownership in the most fundamental way: There is but one name on the title (hence one owner).

Other differences:

- Transfer of the home upon the owner's death proceeds according to will or to the rules of intestacy if no valid will exists.
- If the owner of the house dies, the heir(s) can realize certain capital-gains tax advantages.
- Your home is safe from potential creditors of the spouse whose name is not on the title—assuming

no fraud against creditors is intended when you take title. (In community property states, additional precautions may be necessary to protect your home.)

*Note:* Unless your state has an "equitable distribution" law, a spouse whose name is not on the title will have no claim on the house in the event of a divorce (even if he or she contributed to its purchase). If your only reason for taking title singly is to secure the house against creditors, consider other methods of protection first.

## Your Choice

How do you know which ownership option is right for you?

Each person's situation is different and state laws are not uniform. But here are some thoughts on solutions for situations outside the mainstream of the happily married couple buying their dream house:

- If you're married and have children from previous marriages, taking title can be complex. Tenancy in common would allow you and your spouse to keep distinct ownership shares in the home, which you could pass on to separate heirs. But it offers no solutions to the critical questions: Will the surviving spouse retain full possession of the house during his or her lifetime? If so, who will make the mortgage payments and pay property taxes? If there is a sale, does the surviving spouse share proceeds with the deceased spouse's heirs?
- Singles living together—if committed to each other—may find joint tenancy the best bet because it offers the emotional and financial security of "right of survivorship." But it also provides

an out. If the relationship sours or a career move takes one partner elsewhere, the joint tenancy can be terminated. Keeping the unforeseeable in mind, spell out different ownership percentages clearly on the title.

- Friends or acquaintances who want the tax breaks of home ownership, but can't afford to buy a home on their own, could enter a tenancy in common, an arrangement that can be kept strictly businesslike. Both parties, filing separate returns, can deduct real estate taxes and mortgage interest payments reflecting their ownership percentage and their share of mortgage liability.

# Chapter 11

# How to Cope with a Closing

All the parties were present. The buyer, the seller, the lawyers for both sides, the bank's attorney, and the title agent. They had assembled to transfer a three-year-old contemporary in Chappaqua, New York, from one owner to another. It seemed to be a run-of-the-mill real estate closing.

Just as the contracts were readied for signatures, the buyer exploded, claiming that a washer/dryer offered with the house had been removed from the premises. He wanted $500 to make up for the loss. No check, no closing.

"Time and again, just when you think a closing is in the bag, a problem materializes in the eleventh hour—a problem that threatens to sink the deal," says John Russell, a real estate broker with Holmes & Kennedy. "In this case, it was a buyer who thrived on confrontation and who decided, at the last minute, to angle for something extra.

"Although the seller knew the washer/dryer was never included with the house, he agreed, for the sake of expediency, to meet the buyer's demand. Had he been less flexible, the closing on a $625,000 house would have come unglued over a $500 item."

All too often what appears to be a routine closing turns out to be anything but. Marred by sudden glitches, a one-hour transaction turns into a full-day marathon or even comes apart at the seams, forcing a postponement or even quashing the deal.

But it doesn't have to be that way. Steps can be taken to head off any problems before the day of the closing.

"Let's say you have the worst of all situations: a buyer and a seller who hate each other," Russell says. "If there's something to argue about, the parties will find a way. I've seen raging disputes over pilot lights that don't work and over the amount of fuel left in an oil tank.

"Where it looks as if the buyer and the seller will be at each other's throats, have one of them stay away. Let the seller grant his lawyer a limited power of attorney allowing him to conduct the transaction on his own. Because the principals don't come face-to-face, the closing is more likely to proceed as scheduled."

Here's a checklist of common snags and how to prevent them:

- *Mortgage shortfall*. Assume Smith is buying a $200,000 house, putting down $50,000 and taking out a $150,000 mortgage for the balance. Because his application has been approved, Smith expects the bank to deliver a $150,000 check for the mortgage proceeds at the closing.

  "But the bank," says Hawthorne, New York, lawyer Steven De Young, "may have deducted various costs—including points, legal fees, and tax escrow—from the mortgage proceeds, without informing him in advance. So the buyer finds he has only $142,000. For the deal to proceed, he'll have to make up that shortfall at the closing.

"If he has the money, he may take out his checkbook to cover the balance. But in many cases, the seller won't accept a personal check. If the seller remains adamant about this, and the buyer can't arrange quickly for a certified check, the closing may have to be postponed."

You can prevent this by contacting the bank before the closing date, checking the full amount of the mortgage proceeds, and making certain you'll have enough to pay the seller in full. If there is a shortfall, arrange to cover it with certified funds or a bank check.

"The need for certified funds extends to other costs that may come up at the closing," De Young goes on. "For example, some of the title-insurance companies are now requesting certified checks for their fees. The safest bet is to ask your lawyer how many certified checks you'll need and the exact dollar amount for each. Don't go to the closing without them."

- *Third-party checks.* Quite often, buyers make out checks to themselves with the intention of endorsing them over to the seller at the closing. This is a safety measure: Should the closing be canceled, they're not stuck with funds made out to another party. But some banks are reluctant to honor third-party checks, and the seller may demand a check made out to him or her, rather than one endorsed over by the buyer.

"The issue becomes even more critical when the seller needs the proceeds from the sale to close on a house he's buying later in the same day," De Young explains. "He's not likely to get far with a check written out to one party and then endorsed twice. For that reason, he'll be demanding a clean, certified check written out to him. Unless

the buyer can present this, the closing may have
to be postponed."

• *Liens on the title.* As one of the key players in the
closing process, the title-insurance agent works
behind the scenes checking that the seller owns
the property free and clear. Should there be liens
on the property, they will be discovered during
the title search.

"When people hear the word 'lien,' they think of
something major, like a big bank debt or a court
judgment," says lawyer Peter Bray, president of
West Coast Abstract, a Garden City, New York,
title-insurance agency. "But the lien can be something as minor as an unpaid traffic ticket or a $25
delinquency on a MasterCard. Unless all of these
payments are made and the liens cleared in advance, an escrow account will have to be established at the closing. If this proves impossible, the
closing may have to be adjourned.

"While the liens are generally settled before
the closing, sometimes the small items fall
through the cracks. You can prevent this by asking your lawyer if the title is encumbered, then
acting swiftly to pay off all the lingering obligations."

• *The broken stove.* Fearing leaky basements,
swarms of termites, and ancient furnaces ready to
explode, many buyers hire professional inspectors
to go through the property they want to buy,
checking for damages and defects (see Chapter 9).
If something's wrong with the house, they want to
know about it—and they want the seller to correct it—before the sale is consummated.

"But it doesn't always work that way," says Roy
Cox, president of Amerispec, a home-inspection
service based in Orange, California.

"Typically, the buyer's agreement to purchase a

home is contingent on a favorable inspection. Soon after the contract is signed, the inspector visits the property, checks it over, and issues his report. If there are problems with the house, the seller can agree to make the necessary repairs or the prospective buyer can back out.

"Generally the parties agree on the repairs to be made and the seller sets out to have the work done prior to the buyer's final inspection, known as the 'walk-through.' But this is where things can go wrong.

"If, for one reason or another, the seller doesn't live up to his pledge, and if the buyer discovers that the repairs were not made, the closing will be in jeopardy. This is especially true if the walk-through and the closing are scheduled for the same day. That's because there's no time to fix what's broken before all the parties are scheduled to sit down and finalize the sale.

"Nine times out of ten, there's nothing more devious here than a memory lapse. Before closing on a house I myself was selling, I was supposed to make some minor repairs to a stove clock and a garbage disposal. But it just slipped my mind.

"When I arrived at the closing, the buyer refused to go through with the purchase unless I agreed to escrow $250 for repairs. He was right, of course, so I agreed to the demand and we closed after only a brief delay. But had the problem been more serious, involving a faulty furnace or a hole in the roof, chances are the closing would have been derailed. Some things just don't lend themselves to quick solutions."

To prevent the broken-stove syndrome from upsetting your closing, make a written list of damages and a schedule of dates to have them repaired. Check off each item one at a time, making sure that all work is completed before the buyer's walk-through.

- *Closing costs.* Sometimes there's a gap between the buyer's estimate of the closing costs and what those closing costs really are. Typically, this happens when the buyer misreads the list of projected costs prepared by the bank, or when there is an error in the projections.

"A discrepancy of as little as a quarter percent on the points due at closing can cause a major uproar," Bray says. "The buyer thinks he's been misled and doesn't want to pay a dollar more than he expected. If he's intransigent about this, the closing may be stalled. At the very least it will probably result in a long delay as the buyer and the bank's attorney argue the matter.

"Avoid this by reviewing all the closing costs in advance and having your lawyer verify the figures with the bank. This way there'll be no rude surprises at the closing."

Closing costs may be 5 percent of the purchase price.

- *Shortage of checks.* The universal rule of house closings is that they always require more checks than you think they will. If your best guess calls for 10 checks, bring 15; if you're estimating 15, take 20. Coming up short in the check department may mean the closing cannot proceed.

- *The missing policy.* Before the bank hands over a check for the mortgage proceeds, it will demand an insurance policy or binder, proving that home owner's coverage is in effect at the time of the closing. Failing to obtain the necessary insurance, or to provide proof of coverage, can be a major stumbling block.

"Unless you can run down the street to arrange

for the coverage, you won't be able to close," Russell says. "It's a perfect example of how a minor oversight can jeopardize the entire transaction."

- *The forgotten certificate of occupancy.* Assume the seller built his home five years before, obtained a certificate of occupancy from the town government, and moved into the property as scheduled. Three years later, he added a deck to the house. Unaware that the construction mandated a new certificate of occupancy, he simply left the old one intact.

  "No problem, it seemed, until it came time to sell the house," Russell says. "In the course of the title search, it came to light that the property didn't have a valid certificate of occupancy. Although this should have been taken care of as soon as it was discovered, the seller forgot. When he arrived at the closing, the bank refused to release the mortgage proceeds. The sale had to be postponed."

  Prevent this eleventh-hour nightmare by double-checking that certificates of occupancy have been issued for all additions and improvements to the property.

When it comes to house closings, buyers and sellers will do well to heed Murphy's Law that "if something can go wrong, it probably will."

"The only defense against this is to be a nitpicker," De Young says. "By reviewing every provision and requirement of the closing before you sit down to sign the papers, you'll be forcing the others to do the same. That's the best way to assure that you'll go into the closing and that you'll come out with a sale."

## What Closing Costs Cover

Any closing expenses that a buyer must pay depend on the area of the country. In some areas, sellers pay certain expenses. But here's what you as a buyer may be in for:

**Mortgage application fee:** $100–$300

**Mortgage points:** Each equals 1 percent of the mortgage. These enable the lender to lower the interest rate. Pay for points by a separate check, so you can tax-deduct them for the current year.

**Mortgage insurance:** You might not have to spring for this if you can prove you have enough life insurance already.

**Appraisal:** $125–$200

**Credit report:** $30

**Loan origination fee:** $100–$200

**Inspection reports:** termites ($25–$100); engineer's inspection ($300)

**Title search plus title insurance:** $300–$1,500. (Try to use the seller's title-insurance agency; you might get a discount.)

**Homeowners insurance:** See Chapter 12.

**Recording fee and tax stamps:** They can run up to 0.5 percent of the mortgage amount.

**Lawyers' fees:** The bank's lawyer usually gets $250–$400; yours, up to 1 percent of the price of the house.

**Survey:** $100–$200. But if a survey was made within the past five years, maybe you can skip it. Otherwise, try to have the previous surveyor do it, for a discount.

**Adjustments:** What you owe the seller for taxes he or she has paid past the closing, for oil in the tank, for furnishings or appliances you've bought.

# Chapter 12

# Be Sure You Have the Right Insurance

It's called homeowners, but it protects renters as well, in case their residences are burglarized or are damaged by fire or other disasters. (Unfortunately, only about 20 percent of renters have such insurance.) And, though it may surprise you, homeowners insurance also provides personal-liability coverage—in case you hit someone with a golf ball, or your child breaks a neighbor's window, or your small sailboat crashes into a canoe.

Homeowners insurance comes in "packages," from HO 1 to HO 8. Each protects your home and any detached buildings—along with providing you with personal-liability coverage.

HO 3 is considered preferable to HO 1 and HO 2. HO 5 is "luxury" coverage. HO 4 is for renters. HO 6 for owners of condominiums. HO 8 for owners of houses with lots of gingerbread, like Victorians. You'll never guess what HO 7 covers. Answer: It's not assigned.

A new policy, called the Homeowners Program, provides higher liability protection and higher coverage of items such as jewelry.

You can save up to 20 percent of your premium if you insure a house for only 80 percent of its replacement value. You'll nevertheless receive 100 percent coverage for damage less than 80 percent of the value of the house. (If half of your home is destroyed, you'll receive 50 percent.) But if your house is a total wreck, you'll receive only 80 percent. Still, it's rare for a home to be totally destroyed. Even in a fire, the ground under your house (usually 25 percent of a house's value) will remain, and so will much of the foundation.

The contents of your home automatically receive half the replacement coverage. If your home is insured for $200,000, your possessions will be insured for $100,000. Detached buildings (like a garage or gazebo) will be covered for 10 percent—$20,000. And if your house is uninhabitable after (say) a fire, you'll receive 20 percent for living costs (temporary quarters, and the difference in the cost of meals out versus in)—$40,000.

But anything unusually expensive that you own—like paintings, furs, silverware, or jewelry—won't be adequately covered by your homeowners. Even with the new Homeowners Program, the limit on a fur or jewelry will be $1,000; on silverware and gold, $2,500. So you'll need special "floaters." Cost: $1 to $4 per $100 in value.

Also make sure you have a "replacement cost" rider. If your old moth-eaten carpet is destroyed, for example, you want enough money to buy a new carpet, not just a used one.

Besides homeowners insurance, you may need title insurance. You might live in a state where the ownership of your house may be questioned (perhaps the man who sold you the house didn't reveal that his ex-wife was a co-owner). Also consider insurance against termite damage, which isn't covered by a homeowners

policy and isn't generally tax-deductible. On the West
Coast, inquire about earthquake insurance. Later on,
we'll discuss flood insurance.

Inflation may have raised the cost of rebuilding
your house, so you might need more coverage. Ask
your insurance agent, or a real estate agent, or an
appraiser. You will certainly need more coverage if
you've added improvements, such as extra bathrooms
or bedrooms.

Every few years, inventory the contents of your
house, so you know what's missing in case of a theft.
You might videotape every room, opening cabinet
drawers and closets. Or walk through the house, describing everything into a tape recorder. For expensive items, keep your sales receipts. Store your
records in a safe-deposit box.

You can save on homeowners insurance the same
ways you can on auto insurance. Get three different
prices from insurers. Raise your deductible—to $500,
for example. "The cost of absorbing small losses," says
Norman Hoffman of the College of Insurance in New
York, "will pain you for only a minute." Ask about
discounts if you've installed fire or burglar alarms.
Pay your entire premium annually, if you can swing
it.

If you ever have a claim for over $5,000 and you're
dissatisfied with the settlement an insurance company offers, consider hiring a public adjuster. Adjusters receive 10 to 15 percent of whatever is
recovered. Write to the National Association of Public
Insurance Adjusters, 1613 Munsey Building, Balti-
more, MD 21202.

Where many home owners go wrong is in not having flood insurance, which is not available in standard
homeowners' policies. The only way to cover your
home and possessions is through the National Flood
Insurance Program (NFIP). You don't have to live on a

riverbank or seashore to purchase coverage; it's available to you wherever you live, provided that your community has taken the NFIP's prescribed steps to reduce flood risks.

Nearly 18,000 communities have agreed to participate. About 3,400 are in the initial "emergency" phase of flood management, allowing you to take out limited coverage—up to $35,000 on a single-family home, with another $10,000 policy on its contents. The remaining locales have enacted the required flood-control measures, enabling residents to qualify for the NFIP maximums—$185,000 on homes, another $60,000 on contents. Premiums vary, but average about $250 a year.

Commercial and residential buildings are eligible for even greater coverage. Renters may also take out policies on their possessions.

Flood insurance is required for federal financing—such as FHA- or VA-backed loans—to buy, build, or improve structures in flood-hazard areas of a participating community. Your bank or savings and loan may also require flood coverage before issuing a mortgage.

Information about flood insurance can be obtained from insurance agents who write property and casualty policies. Even though NFIP is a federal program, your insurance agent handles all the paperwork for the policies, collects the premiums, and processes claims. (If there's widespread damage, and the community is declared a disaster area, the government may set up a field office to assist victims with filing claims and applying for emergency loans.)

If you ever have problems, call NFIP's toll-free information number: 1-800-638-6620.

"Take the maximum coverage on both policies—your house and its contents," advises John Abbott (not his real name), who speaks from soggy experience.

"You can't imagine how much damage water can do.

"Flooding was the last thing on our minds when we bought this house 12 years ago," says Abbott, stepping between a pile of lumber and bags of plaster in his suburban Chicago home. "We liked the house and the privacy of a wooded back lot bordering on the river. The water level was well below us and more than 100 yards away. No one around here could even remember that quiet, six-inch-deep stream ever overflowing its banks."

But the rains came. And kept coming. When the Abbotts went to bed one September night, the streets were beginning to fill with water. By 6 A.M., the Des Plaines River was lapping at their doors.

At the peak of the flood, nearly three feet of water stood inside the Abbotts' ranch-style home. It took several days to pump out the murky, smelly liquid. Since the walls were soaked through, everything had to be replaced—paneling, wallboard, insulation, wiring. Carpeting, draperies, furniture, appliances, linens, clothes, and other personal possessions were ruined. For months, the house was uninhabitable, and the Abbott family moved into a motel.

Luckily, the Abbotts had flood insurance to pay for some of the rebuilding and replacement. But too many Americans have no financial protection against flood losses. The Federal Emergency Management Agency estimates that, in an average year, flooding causes about $3 billion in property damage. Two-thirds to three-quarters of these property owners are unprotected. Six million to eight million residences and businesses stand in areas where there is risk of flooding, yet only about two million properties are covered by insurance.

# Chapter 13

# Keeping Burglars at Bay

One out of four residences will be broken into over the next ten years. And, for home owners, it's not only a costly experience. It can be traumatic.

First we'll look at some inexpensive ways to boost the odds against your being victimized. Then we'll get into the area of alarm systems.

Some basic advice:

- Leave a light or radio on when you're not home. Ask neighbors to walk up to your house after a snowfall, to leave footprints.
- Keep your entrance, garage, yard, and porches well lighted.
- Trim bushes and trees, so burglars won't have places to lurk.
- Buy better locks. For standard entrances, check into single- or double-cylinder deadbolts (those that don't spring back). The bolts should extend 1 inch. Buy 3- or 4-inch screws for the strike plates.
- Install key-operated locks for windows. In high-crime areas, put grates or grilles over the windows. Screw a section of hard sheet plastic to the

inside of back-door windows. Put bars on basement windows.
- Vary your routine. Burglars notice if you always leave your home and return at the same time.
- Get a dog with a loud bark.
- Hide jewelry and other valuables in imaginative places. Yes, the refrigerator is a good idea. You and I know about the jewelry-in-the-refrigerator ploy. But most burglars are young—and may *not* know.

According to the Federal Bureau of Investigation, the chances of a burglary—successful or not—drop fifteenfold when a home electronic security system stands guard.

But with all the competing claims of effectiveness and the variety of gadgetry available, how do you choose a system that will protect you?

To find out, we spoke to three experts: the marketing manager of the largest burglar-alarm firm in the country, ADT; a consultant who specializes in unusual installations; and a man who has served time in prison for burglary.

A good home-security system is a balance between making your home impenetrable by a burglar—and still easy to live in. Explains Robert Butchko, marketing manager of ADT, based in Parsippany, New Jersey: "It's easy to make your home practically burglar-proof. The only trouble is that not only will the burglar have a hard time getting in, but so will you."

Home owners must decide how much security they'd like and how much inconvenience they're willing to put up with. Each step up in security means somewhat more inconvenience.

## Your Door Locks

The door lock is a case in point. Many people still don't lock their doors when they leave home: Either they forget, or they just don't bother. And crooks know this only too well. Explains Michael W., the convict, "My experience—and it's been confirmed by my prison buddies—is that many burglars are 'invited' in by the home owner because a door is left unlocked." He says most burglars he has known are discouraged by a locked door: "Why run the risk of breaking in when there are plenty of homes with unlocked front doors?"

Our advisers caution that many ordinary locks provide little protection because they can be opened simply by slipping a plastic card between the door and the jamb to release the spring-loaded bolt. Instead, get a good deadbolt lock backed up with a pry guard—a narrow slab of steel that covers the gap between the door and the jamb to prevent a burglar from forcing the door with a crowbar.

But, says Paul DeMatteis, who heads Counterforce, a New York City firm that installs sophisticated electronic systems in homes and offices, even the best locks are only a deterrent; any determined crook can break down most doors.

## Burglar Alarms

The next line of defense is a burglar alarm. Keep in mind, explains DeMatteis, that the alarm has only two functions: to deter a would-be burglar and, failing that, to warn you or the police that an illegal entry is taking place.

The most basic burglar alarm is an electronic device triggered by the unauthorized opening of a door or window. Typically its controls are inside the house. It gives a home owner a minute or so after opening the door to disarm the alarm by punching in a code.

Such a system can be bought at hardware stores for $100 to $250 and installed by a moderately handy home owner. All our experts caution, though, that such alarms have serious drawbacks: A professional burglar quickly learns to recognize inexpensive or poorly installed alarms and usually can disarm them easily.

At best, do-it-yourself-installed systems are usually effective only for thwarting "casual" thieves, such as local youngsters, who are actually responsible for the majority of burglaries in some neighborhoods.

## A Model Alarm

A good basic electronic alarm should cover all doors and windows. Windows above the first floor can go bare if they are accessible only with a ladder. But if a window can be reached, say, from a tree or a porch roof, it should be protected, too.

Old-style window alarms use two detectors: an electronic trigger that responds to any unauthorized opening, and strips of metal tape along the edges of the glass. Although these are relatively effective, a good second-story burglar would have little trouble cutting the glass without affecting the tape, then disarming the alarm.

More modern window alarms are computer-controlled and use sound sensors as their principal detectors. If a window is opened or the glass broken, the device picks up the "sound signature" and trips the alarm. The computer is so sophisticated that it will ignore a tapping on the window by a child or even a bird; it will respond only to a sound corresponding to a break-in or unauthorized opening.

Crude security systems trigger a loud warning bell to frighten off would-be burglars. Sometimes they are effective, but typically they're ignored by neighbors, the police, and the burglar.

In recent years the strategy of alarm installers has changed. "Today," says DeMatteis, "we focus less on alerting the neighbors and more on scaring the burglar—seeking ways to dissuade him from continuing a break-in." Modern systems trigger a small loudspeaker that announces to the burglar that his presence has been detected, the police have been alerted, and he'd better quit the scene as quickly as possible. They then emit an ear-piercing siren of 140 decibels. The alarm can also be connected to lights in the home, blinking them off and on to frighten the thief.

An even more sophisticated system sends a signal via a small wireless radio transmitter (rather than by telephone, in case the burglar cuts the lines) to a security firm, which then alerts local police. Such a central security service costs between $15 and $28 a month.

If you want even more protection, here's what can be added to any security system:

- *Motion detectors.* If the burglar gets past the door and window alarms, his or her presence will be picked up by a device that looks like an electrical wall outlet, which then sets off the alarm. Such units can be programmed to ignore motions caused by pets or wind.
- *Outdoor detectors.* Like the indoor motion detector, the outdoor device can scan your driveway, front, or backyard. If anyone enters the area, it can be programmed to turn on lights (inside or outside) or broadcast a warning to the intruder.

DeMatteis says many people love this system, not only as a burglar deterrent, but also to illumi-

nate the front of the house when they come home
at night.

- *Screen alarms.* For the home owner who wants to
leave windows open, there are specially designed
screens with built-in detectors that are just as effective as window alarms.

## Advertise Your Alarm

Because the purpose of an alarm is to deter a burglar, it's best to announce that your home is "burglar-
proofed." Apply warning stickers provided by security
companies to conspicuous doors and windows.

Caution: Some home owners, rather than investing
in alarms, buy either a bogus sticker or a device that
looks like an alarm and is bolted onto a front door.
Butchko of ADT warns that such items "may stop a
neighborhood teenager from breaking in, but a professional crook recognizes the real ones from the fakes."

In fact, says ex-burglar Michael, there's an extra
danger in using bogus warnings: "When a thief spots
the fake, he not only knows the house is unprotected,
but that the owner may have something of value he's
trying to protect."

## Oops: False Alarms

A major problem of security systems is false alarms.
Older, less-sophisticated systems frequently are
tripped by wind, dust, or other accidents. Modern systems are not fooled so easily, but problems still occur
occasionally. "For example," says Butchko, "if a crook
tries to break into a house and the alarm fends him
off, the alert will still go to the police. But when they
arrive and find no one there, they assume that the
security system is at fault—and who's to prove otherwise?"

Such "false" alarms cause home owners problems beyond annoyance. Most communities have "false-alarm" ordinances: If an alarm is set off more than a certain number of times and the police find no signs of a break-in, the police will refuse to respond to future alarms until the unit is fully checked out. The resident can be fined as well; the usual fine is $25.

## The Price of Protection

The cost of an effective modern alarm system for a typical three-bedroom suburban home ranges between $1,500 and $3,000. A typical five-room apartment can be protected for about $1,000.

Here's a shopping list of the types of equipment that should be considered for a well-tailored security system:

- The electronic processor: That's the "brains" of the system—a computer that monitors all the sensors, trips the alarms, and shuts them off if the intrusion stops. It includes a keypad panel that permits the home owner to turn on the system, abort it, or even select which rooms to monitor. At night, you may want to activate only the door and window alarms, a motion detector in the foyer and living room, and the yard scanners. If you leave for the weekend, you would want all alarms functioning.

  An effective processor includes a battery backup and an automatic recharging system. Basic price, with a conventional installation, is $600. Extra keypads to control the system from a back door or from your master bedroom (a good idea) cost about $225 each.
- An FM radio transmitter that communicates with a central security telephone for alerting the po-

lice: $225. This extra will cost another $15 to $28 a month in fees.

- Each window sensor costs about $65; if you want the wires hidden, add $10.
- A built-in window screen alarm costs between $75 and $125 each, depending on size and style.
- An outside motion detector, which lights up the area and broadcasts a voice-synthesized warning: about $450.

## Selecting an Installer

Choosing equipment is only half the problem; finding a professional installer is the other half. Many small, fly-by-night firms hastily do several jobs a day. They usually have the worst record for false alarms, and their bankruptcy rate runs to about 20 percent a year.

It's often safer to select a large nationwide firm, but there are advantages to working with a good small firm. The major plus: A technical person, rather than a salesperson, generally will tailor a system to fit your needs, rather than try to sell you a standard package.

At the least, says DeMatteis, check the firm out. Be sure it's bonded, request a list of recent and past customers, and call the customers to ask if they were satisfied. An installer should give you at least a one-year guarantee on installation and equipment.

Should you buy a service contract? Probably not. A good system, after some tuning to get rid of bugs, should operate for 10 years or more without problems.

Also be sure that the installer provides round-the-clock repair service. It doesn't do you any good if the service operates only from 9 to 5 on weekdays. Burglars work extended hours.

# Chapter 14

# Move . . . or Improve?

A few years back, Paul and Carrie Frahm had a problem. Their 3-year-old son, Paul, Jr., would soon be old enough to play in the yard by himself. The trouble was, the Frahms's three-bedroom, split-level home in Wheaton, Illinois, bordered a busy street. "I was terrified of letting him run around outside with all that traffic," Carrie says.

The Frahms decided to move. They chose a bigger house with more amenities. Low interest rates influenced their decision. When they bought their Wheaton home for $58,000 in 1983, the best interest rate they could find was a fixed-rate 12.25 percent. When they applied for a mortgage on their new home, under construction in rural Aurora, rates had dropped to 9.5 percent. That allowed them to trade up from their house, now valued at $79,000, to a $109,000 house.

The new home has four large bedrooms, a bigger kitchen, and an extra half bath. Since the home is on a quiet street, the Frahms don't have to worry about Paul, Jr. playing in traffic.

Although moving to a better neighborhood has always been a part of the American dream, trading up is occurring at a faster pace now than at any time in recent years. The National Association of Realtors estimates that 2.28 million households now switch homes every year.

Low interest rates are one reason. They mean smaller mortgage payments, so buyers can afford more house for less money.

But trading homes can be a traumatic experience, far more exasperating, in some cases, than remodeling to add extra space. For the Frahms, it meant selling their old home before their new home was completed, and moving into an apartment in the interim. For others, it means dealing with clumsy movers and unfamiliar neighborhoods, and discovering all the hidden defects of the new home.

## When Remodeling Makes Sense

A few years ago, Gary and Victoria Bogachus realized that the home that once comfortably accommodated two adults was overwhelmed with the strollers, high chairs, and playpens of one toddler, not to mention another baby on the way.

But the Bellevue, Washington, couple didn't want to move out of their three-bedroom contemporary home, valued at $142,000. "We loved the neighborhood and its proximity to Seattle," says Victoria, an interior designer. Gary, a dentist, needed only five minutes to commute to his office. To buy a larger home would mean moving to the suburbs, where homes cost from $275,000 to $300,000. It would also add 30 minutes to Gary's drive to work.

So the Bogachuses decided to remodel. Four months and $45,000 later, they had a new, spacious family room off the kitchen, with a full bath and storage space. Says Victoria, "We couldn't be more pleased.

Our house is now valued at $175,000, and as far as I'm concerned, we could live here forever if we wanted to."

Jerry and Sharon Riordan added a family room, skylights, and a new kitchen counter and cabinets to their $175,000 Ipswich, Massachusetts, home recently. The project cost them $28,000, but boosted the house's value to $220,000. "We've already recouped the value of our improvements," says Jerry.

These couples' decisions to remodel were economically sound because they followed some important axioms.

Number one: Remodel only if the cost doesn't raise the value of your property more than 20 percent over homes in the area. "No one wants to buy a $120,000 home in a neighborhood of $80,000 homes," says Robert Johnson, executive director of the National Association of Review Appraisers and Mortgage Underwriters. "When people buy a more expensive home, they want a more expensive neighborhood as well." The Bogachus home is one block away from $500,000 homes bordering Lake Washington. The Riordan house was the least expensive house on a block of homes selling for $200,000 to $250,000 each.

Number two: Remodel only if property values are steadily rising. "It's not smart to improve a house that you'll have trouble selling to begin with," says Michael Underhill, a Houston architect and professor at Rice University. The Bogachuses' house in Bellevue has been steadily appreciating about 6 percent a year. The Riordans' house in Ipswich appreciated about 30 percent a year.

Even if houses are appreciating, don't count on getting back your entire investment. Even the most sought-after improvements, such as a remodeled kitchen, may return only about 60 percent of your initial outlay. And to get that, you may have to live in the house at least five more years.

Most experts agree that remodeling is most successful when the home owner wants only one major change in the house. "If you start monkeying around with a lot of changes, the bills really pile up," says James B. Warkentin, a real estate counselor in Springfield, Virginia. For resale value, experts say that you should confine remodeling to projects that improve or increase the core space in your home— kitchens, living rooms, family rooms, and dining areas.

Also resist the urge to incorporate highly personalized designs that prospective buyers may not find suitable—a futuristic high-tech bathroom in a Colonial home, for example. Says Warkentin, "If you break tradition with your house's style, you do it at your own risk."

Keep in mind that remodeling can be every bit as stressful as moving. You'll need building permits. You'll have to notify your insurance company that you're making additions to your home. The town's zoning rules will need checking to see if you can build on your lot. You may have to hire a general contractor, and perhaps even an architect if the project will alter the outside appearance of your home. You'll probably want to obtain a second mortgage.

You'll also have to be prepared to devote several months of your life to overseeing the activity every step of the way. "It takes 12 to 16 weeks to add on a room," says Jack Bloodgood, an architect in Des Moines, Iowa. "Contractors will tell you it takes eight weeks, but they tend to underestimate."

Then there are the special problems that you can't plan for. If your house was built before 1950, adding on a new bedroom may put too much strain on your electrical system. Just to bring in the extra electrical service from the street could cost $2,000. If the house inspector finds that the entire home's wiring is insufficient to support the service, you might have to rewire the entire house.

And, of course, remodeling can only solve problems within your house. If the neighborhood is becoming too built up, or the schools are deteriorating, remodeling for any reason other than your personal comfort is a waste of money. "You're better off if you take the money you would have spent remodeling, add it to your home's equity, and see what it will buy you elsewhere," Johnson says.

## When It Pays to Move

Americans, on average, move about once every eight years. Some 40 percent of home buyers cite the need for additional space as one of their main reasons, according to the National Association of Realtors.

But moving, like remodeling, makes economic sense only under the right conditions. The first is that you're getting something more or better than what you're giving up, whether that's a newer, more energy-efficient home, a better school district, or a shorter commute to work. "There are trade-offs in a move. You may give up a short commute to work for a larger home, but the important thing is that you know what you're giving up and what you're getting," says John Weidlein of the National Homeowners Association.

That's why it's crucial to look at more than just the price of the house when you trade up.

Compare property tax rates. Will you have to pay a much larger bill in your new home?

How about commuting costs? An extra $4 each day can add up to $1,000 a year.

Then there's the question of neighborhood stability. If you're moving from an older, established neighborhood into a new community, are schools and sanitation, police, and fire services as good as in your old community?

Will your homeowners insurance cost more? Will you need to join special clubs, hire a landscaper, or purchase new furniture just to fit into the neighborhood?

Since moving involves a lot of expenses (typically a 6 percent commission for selling your house, 5 percent closing costs on a new home, and $1,000 or more in moving expenses), make certain the value of the move outweighs these expenses. Moving to a new home because you don't want to pay $20,000 to build a family room in your old home doesn't make sense if you'll have to put $20,000 into the new home's outmoded kitchen.

Do consider moving, however, if the value of real estate in your area has plateaued, and you can afford to buy in a better neighborhood that's still on the rise. In that case, it pays to take your gains while you can, and trade up to a home with more up-side potential. This is especially true if you can afford a custom-built, luxury property in a prime location. If the housing market turns down in the future, a splendid home in a premium area will probably hold its value better than a run-of-the-mill house.

Even if moving up to a three-bedroom house will cost you slightly more than adding another bedroom to your current house, remodelers and real estate agents alike believe you should probably make the move, given today's economic climate. "The difference between a two-bedroom and a three-bedroom house isn't just one bedroom," says Bloodgood. "It's the size of the living room, the counter space in the kitchen, and the number of bathrooms."

## What Financing Will Cost You

If you're planning to remodel, you have a number of options for financing. Unless your current mortgage carries an interest rate 2 or more percentage points higher than current rates, it's generally best not to refinance.

If your company has a profit-sharing plan, or you own a whole-life insurance policy, consider borrowing from these sources first, because you can probably get below-market rates and you won't have to pay any up-front fees.

The next-best thing is to open a home equity line of credit at a bank, brokerage house, savings and loan association, or credit union. That will allow you to borrow up to 70 or 80 percent of the value of the equity in your house. Because most equity lines carry an adjustable interest rate and charge interest only on the outstanding balance, they can be cheaper than a second mortgage for a fixed amount of money at a fixed rate of interest. Expect to pay closing costs, including points, and perhaps a percentage point more interest than you would on a first mortgage.

One person you *shouldn't* borrow from is your remodeler. Remodelers' terms and rates are usually steeper than you can get elsewhere.

If you're trading homes, you'll have to pay any expenses associated with closing out your old mortgage, plus the costs of obtaining a new mortgage. These costs may include a title search, appraisal fee, points, and costs to record deeds.

Even with a low mortgage rate, figure on paying about 2 percentage points more than the stated interest rate the first year of your mortgage, when you add in these closing costs. Then there's the cost of a bridge loan, if you plan to move into your house before your old home is sold. This can add several hundred dollars onto your moving costs, depending on how long it takes to sell your old home.

# Chapter 15

# Choosing a Remodeler

Wanda Filipkowski's daughter, Joanne, was married recently and faced the typical New Yorker's dilemma: Housing prices were astronomical, and she and her husband couldn't afford anything halfway decent. Wanda came to the rescue: "I'll have a second story built on my own house," she told them. "You two pay the cost, live here, and own half the house, too."

Joanne and Diego leaped at the idea. The cost wasn't intimidating: $50,000 for three bedrooms, a living room, a dining room, a bathroom, and a kitchen.

"It's a bargain because they don't have to buy any land," Mrs. Filipkowski explains. "My only worry is that everyone keeps telling me terrible stories about contractors...."

Although many remodelers (also called general contractors) are conscientious and competent, almost every customer has gripes about delays, overcharges, and shoddy materials and workmanship.

In most states, anyone can set up shop as a remodeler. "A carpenter who has repaneled a room may buy himself a pickup truck and power saw, buy a big ad in the Yellow Pages, and await your phone call to have your kitchen renovated," says a real estate broker in the Midwest. "I attended my twentieth high-school class reunion a few weeks ago, and all the guys I remember as hoods now call themselves general contractors."

But if you go about remodeling carefully, the only painful part may be the checks you must write. Just accept two facts beforehand: It will cost more and take longer than you think.

Still, you may get some fun out of it. "We had a guy add a room onto our house," says a physician's wife in St. Louis. "He was wonderful, but the only people helping him were a drug addict, who happened to be his brother-in-law, and another yo-yo. He ended up working alone, and it took six months for him, working every day, to finish. The plus side is that he was good at taking phone messages and baby-sitting for the kids. We got used to having him around. Now even the dog misses him."

## Be Your Own General Contractor?

Should you go it alone, hiring subcontractors such as electricians and carpenters and plumbers, and supervising their work? You can save the 10 to 20 percent fee that a general contractor would charge. But is it worth it? You need to be efficient, have spare time, abundant patience, be prepared to stay home from work, and know trustworthy tradespeople.

You'll also have to have workers' compensation insurance (ask your agent) and building permits; select and schedule the delivery of materials; check the zoning code to see whether, for example, a second-story addition must be set back farther from the street than the first floor; and study the building code (can you use plastic pipes for your plumbing?).

"There's no reason why anyone can't be the general contractor on a remodeling job if you're willing to play hardball with those bozos," says Kris Hallam, a medical journal editor who is renovating a brownstone in Brooklyn, New York. "And you have to be tough. One guy tried to hit us with an extra $500 for fixing a fireplace, although it was included in the estimate." Her experience leads her to suggest: "You'll also have to be able to take off some time from work—or leave your keys with a neighbor, and later on change the locks."

Arthur M. Watkins, a writer and housing authority, believes that it's easier to be your own general contractor on a new house rather than an old one, because of the unexpected problems remodeling may present. Studs, for example, are 15 inches apart in new construction, but may be closer, or farther, in older buildings.

Unless you have the skills, time, strength, special tools, and interest, limit your do-it-yourself efforts to painting and carting debris. Even that will cut costs somewhat, and should give you and your family a feeling of satisfaction.

## Finding a General Contractor

Reports Shirley Fitzpatrick of Hillsdale, New Jersey: "We picked a man from the Yellow Pages to remodel the bathroom. He had big advertisements and his own radio-dispatched trucks. My husband ripped out all the fixtures before the plumber arrived. He wasn't there five minutes when the plumbing inspector arrived. He had seen the truck, knew the plumber wasn't licensed in Hillsdale, and threw him off the job! We had three little children at the time, and without that bathroom, we had to move in with relatives for two weeks. And we had a heck of a time getting a new plumber."

Horror stories abound, so if you don't make the effort to find a good general contractor, you may wind

may do a poor job on his first or second bathroom. In general, choose a big company over a little one. If a big company makes a mistake and underestimates the cost of one job, it can survive. A small company might cut costs at your expense.

Never choose a contractor because he or she comes cheap. Says Distasio, "A very low estimate may mean bad materials and good workmen, good materials and bad workmen, or—worst of all—bad materials and bad workmen." NARI reports that more than 80 percent of the complaints it receives come from customers who "thought they were getting a bargain price."

## Getting Bids

Have the remodeler you have confidence in list the specifications (what you'll need, how much, and the brand names). Then have your other candidates submit bids on the same specs.

If the job is costly, obtain three to six bids. The bid itself should bear the contractors' insurance numbers for liability and worker's compensation insurance.

Besides a low price, look for a warranty on the work done. Some contractors offer five-year warranties; the least you should accept is a year.

Once you have the bids in hand, show the contractor with the best reputation the competing bids, assuming that they're lower. See if he or she will agree to come down a bit. Of course, if two contractors with comparable reputations submit markedly different bids, choose the one whose bid is lower.

## The Contract

Many remodelers suggest "cost-plus" contracts, but be on your guard unless you're dealing with someone you really trust. Their profit—10 percent, say—depends on what the materials cost. But read your contract carefully. One physician found that his contractor had bought the most expensive materials, just to increase his profit, and had also included, as costs, a $500 weekly salary for himself and $250 for his secretary!

If you trust a remodeler, a cost-plus contract may be appropriate. But set a maximum: If the cost turns out to be less, you will pocket the difference. The contractor should agree to give you a bill, marked paid, for all materials, and a record of the time each worker put in.

The best rule about contracts with remodelers may be the one that Patrick Distasio himself mentions: "Pay them slow."

Typical contracts ask that you pay one-third of the total price at the beginning, one-third halfway, and one-third at the end. But it's better to pay as little as possible up front.

"I'd worry if it's more than 10 percent," says Hollye Fisk, an architect-turned-lawyer in Dallas. "If it's more than 10 percent, the contractor may just pocket the money and walk away with it." He also urges that you pay the contractor month by month, after seeing the bills for materials and for the subcontractors. "Any reputable contractor who's not desperate for money will accept this arrangement," Fisk says. "It's standard in commercial construction."

He also suggests that you not pay any bills unless you receive statements from all subcontractors that they've been paid to date.

Finally, hold back at least 15 percent of the total price until the job is finished, you've tested everything, and the place has been cleaned up.

A good contract describes how debris will be removed, how house furnishings will be protected, what work you will do yourself, how changes will be handled, when the work will start and when it will end, what happens if you are dissatisfied and want to cancel the contract, and the protection you have against property liens that subcontractors might lodge against you if the general contractor doesn't pay them.

The contract should mention the plans and the specs, and—to make them official—they should be attached to the contract.

If you must obtain financing first, specify that the contract will not take effect unless you obtain a loan at a particular interest rate within two weeks (or whenever).

Don't be shy about suggesting changes in the contract. A conscientious remodeler will have no reason to complain if your changes are fair.

During construction, check that the materials are exactly what they are supposed to be, and do it every day. Don't rely on a building inspector to keep the workers honest. Says architect Doug Walter of Denver, "A building inspector just looks for gross errors, not whether the lumber is the cheap 'standard' or whether it's good 'commercial' grade."

Do some homework, too. Read articles and books about the kind of remodeling you're having done, so you know how to evaluate the work—such as which windows are made by the leading firms, how siding should be installed (the fittings should be tight), how many electrical outlets a wall should have (at least one every 12 feet).

# Chapter 16

# Moving Need Not Be Traumatic

Moving day is approaching. You've packed most of your belongings, sent change-of-address cards to friends, family, and colleagues, arranged to cancel utilities, done last-minute chores such as picking up clothes from the cleaners and returning library books and rented videotapes. You even opened a checking account in your new city, so you'll have funds on hand when you arrive. Ready to move? Not quite.

You probably have more loose ends to tie up than you imagine. The following checklist, compiled with the aid of relocation specialist Jan Dickinson and other experts, can help you make all the right moves:

- Notify all departments of your bank of your change of address, and be sure to include numbers of all accounts—checking, savings (even the small one that's been gathering dust), IRAs, and Keoghs.
- Remove the contents of your safe-deposit box.
- Close all local charge accounts and pay off outstanding balances in stores where you maintain a line of credit. If you have items on a layaway

plan, pay the balance in full or make other arrangements with your creditor.

- Clear any tax assessments against your home.
- Check your credit history to be sure all information is correct. (The bank where you have your checking account can probably tell you which credit bureau or bureaus have your file.)
- Inform major credit-card companies of your move by completing the change-of-address section on your most recent bills.
- Promptly notify any creditor who will tack on interest or other charges if bills are delayed in transit.
- Tell people who owe you money about your move.
- Collect utilities deposits and the security deposit if you're leaving an apartment.
- Notify business and professional organizations to which you pay dues annually. Resign from local chapters, or transfer your membership to your new location.
- Review your car insurance policy and check with your agent to find out how your premium will be affected. If you're financing a car, discuss your move with the lending institution to determine whether you can transfer title to your new state.
- Notify your automobile club.
- Inform your local Social Security office to avoid delays in receiving any retirement, disability, survivor's benefits, or other income due you.
- Inform the Internal Revenue Service and your state and city tax offices of your move, especially if you're waiting for a refund.
- Send a change-of-address form to any former employers who will be sending you W-2 forms at the end of the year. If you're self-employed in a service business or have earned tips or commissions, inform customers who send you 1099 forms. Also,

alert former employers of companies where you participate in profit-sharing or pension funds.

- Tell your broker of your move, and decide whether to continue your relationship or move to a new branch or brokerage house. Also alert companies in which you own stock to send dividends to your new address. If you are receiving dividends from a life insurance policy, notify that company as well.

- Discuss your move with your lawyer to determine whether you need a new will (state laws vary). Also review your choice of executor.

- Notify the family court if you pay or receive child support or alimony.

- Live-togethers should check cohabitation laws if moving to a new state.

- Determine how service contracts on appliances or home business equipment will be affected. If the contract is held by the manufacturer, notify the company and find out the name of a local service outlet. If you have a store-backed contract, find out whether there is a branch in your new location that will honor the contract.

- Check with your health insurance company to see whether your family's coverage will be affected by your move.

- Have medical and dental records, for all members of your family, forwarded to health professionals in your new city, or take copies of the records with you. Don't forget school immunization records for your children.

- Get copies of medical and immunization records for your pets.

- Refill prescriptions for any medicine you or members of your family take regularly.

- Obtain copies of prescriptions for contact lenses

and eyeglasses from your eye doctor or optome-
trist.

- If you and your spouse plan to set up your new home before sending for your children, complete emergency medical-authorization forms for the person who will be caring for your children, so they can be treated in case of accident or injury.
- Obtain copies of birth and baptism certificates for all members of your family.
- If you or your children are registered with the local draft board, inform the board of your move.
- Try to sell the remainder of your country club or health club memberships.
- If you have season tickets for sporting events or the theater, sell them or give them to friends.
- Notify the police if your home will be vacant for any period of time during your move.
- Take your local phone directory with you when you move. If you've overlooked anything, you'll be able to contact the appropriate person promptly.
- Notify your post office to forward your mail.

# Chapter 17

# Dress Up Your Home
# for Resale

Before you put your house on the market, give it "curb appeal." That's the way to ensure a prospective buyer's immediate positive impression of your house.

If two identical houses in the same neighborhood go on sale simultaneously, the better prepared of the two will sell faster. And Realtors agree that a spruced-up house commands a higher sales price than its run-down counterpart.

How do you create curb appeal?

Look at your home and property objectively. List all the readily apparent problems and estimate how long and how much money it will take to correct each one.

Assign a priority to each problem listed. Most important for buyer appeal is to take care of loose shingles or tiles; cracked pavements; broken doorknobs; leaky faucets; sticky doors and windows; warped cabinet drawers; torn screens; dirty walls, floors, and doors; blown light bulbs; curling, dull, dirty wallpaper—and anything else awry at eye level.

Make a realistic evaluation of these chores. What you can't handle, hire someone else to do.

Appraise your shrubbery, lawn, and gardens. Are

there colorful plants around that perk up the garden's appeal?

Do the cosmetic jobs (painting, for example) last, so the wear and tear of normal living won't undo what you have completed.

Painting is an especially effective spruce-up. A coat of paint can double the value of the house.

Keep the house neat. Bathrooms and kitchens should sparkle, because these two areas sell homes. Tidy and orderly closets give the appearance of being larger. But don't get neurotic about neatness. Prospective buyers expect to see a lived-in look—just not too much of it. And keep the kids out of sight when potential buyers are expected.

# Chapter 18

# Selling Your Home without a Broker

Selling your house yourself does have drawbacks.

You have to remain at home and escort strangers through your house. Some visitors may be sightseers, not interested buyers. Some may not even be able to afford your house. A few may be given to lifting nice things they see during their tour. You have to be honest about any major defects in your house, such as a leaky roof, lest you be sued later on.

Even so, many people who successfully sell their own houses report that it was not only a piece of cake, but a lot of fun besides. Recently we interviewed people across the country who sold or are trying to sell their houses without brokers. Here's the advice they have for other sell-it-yourselfers:

- *Consider a fact sheet.* When she was selling her house on Long Island, Joyce Kaye of New York City did something other home owners might emulate. She handed out copies of a fact sheet describing the house. "Even brokers who saw the sheet were surprised," she says. The fact sheet carried a photograph of the house, a description of its best features (like a central vacuum), and details about operating expenses and the proximity of schools and public transportation. Everyone who visited the house in West Babylon, New York, was handed a copy, so when they returned home, they had more than just a vague memory of the house.

Kaye had bought the house when she was 24. "I felt real proud, being a single woman buying my own place," she recalls. But because she works in Manhattan, she took an apartment there.

She decided to sell the house herself, without a broker, because, she says, "I wasn't going to give the keys to a Realtor to show to people while I wasn't home. I figured, if I'm going to be home anyway, why not eliminate the third party and save the commission?" She wasn't intimidated by the prospect. "I'm not normally the type of person who is intimidated."

From her bank she obtained the name of a real estate appraiser, who charged her $175 to suggest a price for her house. He also drove her past other neighborhood houses that had sold recently, and told her their sale prices. Then, on her own, she asked three real estate firms to tell her the market price of her house, which they did without charge. With four prices now, she chose one in the middle: $67,000.

Next, she trimmed the hedges around the house. "I didn't have the house painted," she says. "In general, it was in very good condition."

Then she placed ads in the local daily newspaper, which cost $120 a week. The ad stressed the house's remodeled kitchen and the sewer hookup (many houses in the area have only septic tank systems). And she scheduled an open house from 10 A.M. to 4 P.M. on a Saturday.

A lot of people showed up, but no one was interested. Kaye had made a mistake: She had not included her phone number in the advertisement. People could not call to find out more details— details that might have saved them a visit, and spared Kaye the trouble of showing them around.

She placed a second ad, giving her phone number. And instead of an open house, she scheduled appointments, so she didn't have to stay home all day.

Although her ad said "principals only," about 15 brokers called. "But I had an answering machine on during the day, so if a broker called and left a name, I just didn't call back," says Kaye. "The answering machine was fantastic! I couldn't have sold my house without it."

Late one afternoon, a builder came by with his wife. "As soon as she saw the kitchen, she said, 'It fits. We can stop looking.'" They put down a $100 binder (Kaye should not have accepted so little— 10 percent of the sale price is standard), and they both retained lawyers. The house sold for exactly what Kaye was asking.

Was she worried about her safety—a single woman alone in a house letting strangers in? She pauses. "I never even thought of it," she says finally. "It's a nice, safe neighborhood." As for possible pilfering, "I took a chance, I guess. Maybe I'm naive. But I didn't have anything of value there."

Did she have any unpleasant surprises selling her own house? "The only surprise came when someone asked me whether the house had 120–220 wiring. I had no idea. We had to look at the electrical box."

Was she prepared to list the house with a broker if it had not sold quickly? "I thought I'd give it a month. But I had no doubt I'd be able to sell it. It was a good price."

- *Write a fact-filled advertisement.* Don Cowan of Lexington, Kentucky, had not sold his house when we spoke with him, but he is blessed with two advantages that most sell-it-yourselfers do not have. He works for a local newspaper and can place advertisements free of charge. And he works in the advertising department, so he knows how to write a good ad. His read:

> (Homes for Sale)
> Eastlake/Century Hills Contemporary starter home, skylights, fireplace, heatpump, central air, great room with loft. Cul-de-sac. 2 years old. $46,000. 272-1391. Nights and weekends.

Readership studies have found, he says, that home buyers want to know the price, the location, the number of square feet, the number of bedrooms, and possible financing. (But, he adds, it's best to include these features only if they are strong selling points.) After listing these basics, he says, stress whatever special features the house has, such as fireplace or central air-conditioning. (A "great room" is a combination living and dining room.)

Cowan derides ads—some written by brokers —that get flowery and suggest that people can nestle up close to their fireplace. "I believe in being straightforward."

He also thinks you should be specific, even if you fear that some buyers will be turned off. A house feature that discourages one person may attract another. Some people don't want a garage attached to the house, because they think gas fumes will spread into the rooms. Others like the idea of carrying groceries from a car directly into the house in cold weather. By being specific in your ad, you can weed out buyers who would not have purchased your house anyway.

"If you don't mention something," Cowan adds, "some readers may figure the worst." If you skip over such basics as the number of bedrooms, for instance, readers may think that a house has only two.

- *Ensure your safety.* Linda Larson of Sandy, Utah (near Salt Lake City), tried to arrange appointments with buyers only when her husband Larry was at home. Sometimes Larry, a labor contractor, was just not available. She showed the house anyway, "with two Dobermans at my side."

  Several years ago, the Larsons successfully sold a house without a broker. Last time, they called in an appraiser; this time, they just asked neighbors who were selling their houses what they were asking. The Larsons settled upon $87,500.

  They had some rooms repainted and some carpeting replaced, then ran an ad in the local daily for four days, for $13. She had modeled her newspaper ad after others she had seen:

  By owner in Sandy, 1,900 sq. ft. 3 bdrms, 2 baths. Fireplace and woodburning stove in fin. basement. Fully landscaped and fenced ½ acre horse property. Many extras! $87,500. Call 571–9490 to see!

- *Don't get discouraged quickly.* The first day that Debbie Neumayer, a homemaker in Glen View, Illinois, ran an ad in local newspapers about her house, she didn't receive a single phone call.

  But that weekend, 18 people came to Mrs. Neumayer's open house. She and her husband

Charles, who owns a gas station, sold their house two weeks later. Mrs. Neumayer's advice to other sell-it-yourselfers: "Give yourself at least a month. It's too easy to let brokers talk you into signing with them."

To set a price, the Neumayers called in four brokers. "Around here, everyone wants to give you a free market evaluation," she reports. The lowest price was $115,000; the highest $129,000. They settled on $120,000.

Next, they filled in cracks with plaster of paris, painted, put children's toys away, and cleared out crowded closets. "We did what we do when company is coming." They collected data on taxes and heating costs, and prepared a fact sheet.

They also put up for-sale signs at busy intersections nearby, and spent $200 on ads in local newspapers.

To ensure her safety, Mrs. Neumayer arranged for several people to come at the same time. She also had put away anything valuable, "but I didn't worry about it."

The woman who bought the house—for $120,000—already owned a house, so the Neumayers felt they didn't have to worry about her ability to afford theirs.

Was there anything she didn't like about selling her house by herself?

Says Mrs. Neumayer, "There *were* no drawbacks. I didn't mind waiting for people to show up. And, in two weeks, I saved $7,000. Thank heavens I didn't get discouraged!"

- *Consider a discount broker.* People dubious about selling their houses without brokers can compromise. They can choose a discount broker—someone who charges much less than the going rates of 5 to 7 percent, but who also does less work.

James and Sandy Jones (not their real names) of Barrington, Rhode Island, were planning to sell their house without a broker, but then spotted a newspaper ad for a discount broker. The broker would charge just 1.5 percent of the sales price, screen prospective buyers, and handle the paper- work—but not show the house. Mrs. Jones called him.

The Joneses—he is a 45-year-old investment manager, she is 44—feel that brokers' fees are too high. They thought their house was worth about $200,000, and that a $12,000 broker's fee was too high for a house they felt would sell itself. "Brokers claim that their fees are negotiable," Mrs. Jones says, "but it always winds up being 6 or 7 percent."

Once they decided on a discount broker, the Joneses set a price on their house. "We had lived in the area for seven years," Mrs. Jones says, "and we were familiar with the market." The discount broker agreed that their price of $200,000 was reasonable.

She placed an ad stressing the house's best fea- tures—Colonial style, brick frame, center hall, the family room in the basement, the brick patio, the slate roof, and so forth. They had decided that Mrs. Jones would *not* show the house herself, without her husband, "if I didn't have a good feel- ing about the people."

Just about that time, a friend of the Joneses was playing tennis with someone, and happened to mention that he knew of a house for sale. The other tennis player was interested. He and his wife came right over. "They loved it and wanted it—and they didn't want to lose it," says Mrs. Jones. "They offered $210,000, all in cash. And since we hadn't actually signed with the discount broker, all that money was ours."

## What You Can Save

These days, houses typically sell for $90,000 to $100,000. If you can skip a 6 or 7 percent broker's commission, you'll save around $6,000, minus—to give a somewhat extravagant figure—$500 for newspaper ads.

Let's suppose it takes you 40 working hours to sell your house. The $5,500 you save, divided by 40 hours, translates into $137.50 an hour, $4,400 a week, $286,000 a year.

It might be argued, of course, that the buyer—not the seller—actually pays the broker's commission, because it's supposedly factored into the market price of the house. But if you can sell your house for what it would have sold for with a broker, you will save the entire commission. And if you decide to split the typical $5,500 commission with the buyer by lowering your price by $2,750, you will nonetheless wind up being compensated at a rate of $143,000 a year. The fact that your house is somewhat underpriced may also enable you to sell it more quickly than you would have with a broker.

# Chapter 19

# Buying Resort Property

Buying a resort property in a scenic locale for investment and enjoyment now, with the long-term goal of making it your retirement home, sounds like having your cake and eating it, too.

For psychologist Henry Singer of Westport, Connecticut, every bite of the cake has been delicious.

Dr. Singer and his wife, Rosina, bought a Florida vacation condominium in 1981 with a triple purpose in mind. "Inflation was still rampant," he recalls, "and we thought an income-producing recreational property would be a hedge against inflation, a good place to spend our vacations and, at the same time, an investment in our future retirement."

Because of their long-term retirement goals, the Singers had certain items on their property shopping list:

- A year-round warm climate
- A condominium, not another house, to reduce up-keep and maintenance
- A development with a good population mix—not just retirees, but people and families of all ages
- A bustling town or city nearby

- A natural-looking community
- A locale with rental potential; that is, at least one strong "season"
- Easy access by air from the New York City area

They discovered the Pelican Cove condominium outside Sarasota, Florida, which they bought, partly by chance.

They found it en route to a vacation at Captiva Island, Florida. A friend asked them to look at a place he had heard about near Sarasota. Since their plane stopped at Sarasota, they decided to check it out.

Both the area and the development intrigued them. "We responded immediately to the quality of life there," he says. "Sarasota seemed to be bubbling with activity, and the development itself was along a quiet bay. No building in the complex was over two stories, and everything was set under flowering orange, lemon, and grapefruit trees. It seemed to be one of those rare Florida developments that considered the natural environment a part of its ambience."

The Singers collected information for their friends, then spent much of their spare time that year looking at various Florida condominiums. But their thoughts kept returning to Pelican Cove.

Meanwhile, their friends had visited Pelican Cove and decided to buy two units. They persuaded the Singers that, if they were going to buy, this was the time. By negotiating together for their separate units, Henry and his friend got a package deal from the developer, with a 5 percent discount on each unit, along with an additional 5 percent preconstruction discount.

Henry negotiated with a local bank for a variable-rate mortgage for three years, instead of a conventional fixed-rate, 30-year mortgage.

The Singers bought into a lively, arts-minded community. "The human factor is an intangible you really can't put into your shopping list," says Rosina, "but it's a welcome 'extra' when it happens, and it's particularly pleasing if you plan to retire in a community."

Because the Singers bought one of the last units to be built in the complex, the appreciation on their unit hasn't matched that of earlier purchasers. Their $80,000 two-bedroom, two-bath, two-porch unit would have cost them $50,000 if they had bought it three years earlier. Today's purchasers will find a similar Pelican Cove villa for resale at $100,000 or more.

In addition to the $20,000 appreciation, there have been considerable tax advantages.

Because the Singers rent out their condominium, they are able to depreciate the cost. They are also permitted numerous deductions on their income tax for some, if not all, of their operating expenses, maintenance and repair costs, management fees, rental agency fees and commissions, advertisements for rentals, two trips a year to inspect and prepare the property for rentals, and real estate taxes.

To claim all the operating cost deductions, together with such expenses as interest, property taxes, and casualty losses, the Singers can use their condominium only a limited number of days per year, based on an IRS formula. The formula for personal use depends on the number of days the unit is rented. Maximum personal use is up to 14 days if the unit is rented between 15 and 149 days; or up to 10 percent of rental days if they total 150 or more. Some extra days are permitted to the owner for legitimate repairs, maintenance, and preparing the unit for rental.

Various carrying charges cost the Singers about $900 per month, or $10,800 per year. These charges include the interest on their mortgage and a regime fee, which encompasses building maintenance, landscaping, pest control, taxes, electricity, management fee, insurance (property, flood, liability), and a reserve for replacement of major structural elements, such as roofs.

These annual charges have been more than offset by the combination of deductions, depreciation, and rentals, which totals between $12,000 and $13,000 annually. Although rentals have not been as regular as the Singers had hoped, they have helped. "Rentals are just part of the depreciation-deduction-sheltering package. If you buy a resort condo thinking the rentals alone will turn a profit," Singer says, "you may be deluding yourself. It rarely happens that way."

During the first three years they owned it, the Singers rented their condominium as often as possible, took all their IRS-allowable deductions, and spent the maximum time permitted them under IRS regulations.

But now the Singers have decided to forgo the extra deductions and to spend more time at their Pelican Cove condo.

"We're inching our way toward retirement, trying to see what it's like living there for a sizable stretch of time." Henry, who is the director of the Human Resources Institute in Westport, has no specific retirement date targeted. "Our tentative plan is to keep our Westport house because the mortgage is virtually paid up, and use it as a summer house, making Pelican Cove our permanent home. Not only do we like those Florida winters, but we like the state's laws on inheritance taxes and dividends." (Florida has no personal income tax and no inheritance tax.)

First-time resort property buyers, especially those in search of retirement property, should:

- Investigate the area carefully. Is it a place where you will want to spend much of the rest of your life? Are there amenities, amusements, activities nearby? Is the area on the way up or down? Check on the cost of living. Compare prices for groceries, restaurants, shops. Will the area be too expensive for your retirement income?
- Check the track record of the builder to see if he or she is likely to deliver on promises. Read the prospectus carefully.
- As a rule of thumb, property on the waterfront in a given development is a better investment (and has greater rental potential) than inland property in the same development, even though it is usually more expensive. But before buying, check on pollution control of the water and possible soil or beach erosion.
- Study the property itself. Is routine maintenance up to par? Are the grounds, roads, and facilities well-kept? Check built-in fire warning, control, and escape mechanisms at the complex itself.
- Check the entire property map for additional (but negative) development potential possibilities. The view of the ocean from your unit's terrace may be stupendous at this moment, but if there is an empty lot in front of you, you may be facing a new unit before long. Get protection in your contract, not by words alone.
- Consider the recreational facilities available. Are there enough swimming pools for the number of residents in the complex? Are golf, tennis, and other sports available? At what extra charge? Are the facilities owned by the condominium complex? If leased, can fees be boosted without owners' approval? (This was the subject of developers' rip-offs in the past in many recreational areas,

especially in Florida.) Can your renters use the facilities without charge or at a modest fee? The more recreational possibilities available, the greater the rental potential.

- Consider the accessibility of the complex. Is it a short drive from a major airport, or does it require hours or days to reach? Are there bus routes or taxis nearby? Rentals and possible resale are easier if quick access is available. How about proximity to health facilities?

- Security is important in a resort complex. Is the area well protected? How about protection against natural hazards: floods, hurricanes, or avalanches? What would such a catastrophe do to your investment? What kind of insurance is necessary?

These are all questions to be asked and sorted out before you buy. But for many people, the all-important question is where to buy.

The final decision depends on you and what appeals to you—in climate, terrain, and ambience. What, where, and how well you choose may make your decision truly the most important first day of the rest of your life.

Keep an eye on:

1. Quality. A developer will almost always try to provide the least-expensive items he or she can. It is up to you, the buyer, to insist on a better grade of carpet, higher quality light fixtures, and a better air-conditioning unit and appliance package—before you sign on the dotted line. Bargain, bargain, bargain.

2. The financial clout of the developer. It's advisable to enlist the developer's help in obtaining

the best possible mortgage rate. In most resort areas, a buyer must use a local bank. The developer has a vested interest in closing the deal, so get him or her working to help you find the bank with the best interest rate. Make that part of your bargaining wedge, too.

# Chapter 20

# Tax Angles

### Uncle Sam Loves Home Owners

The tax benefits of owning your own home—or condominium, cooperative, houseboat, whatever—have been crimped by tax reform, but definitely not eliminated.

Home owners still enjoy wonderful deductions that renters don't—for payments for state and local real estate taxes, and (with possible limits) mortgage interest payments. (A deduction is an amount of money you subtract from your taxable income, so you wind up paying less taxes. But you can use such deductions only if you "itemize"—list all your deductions instead of taking a flat amount, the "standard deduction.")

What's more, there's a cornucopia of other blessings that Uncle Sam bestows upon home owners, just to encourage Americans to join the club.

For instance: If a home owner decides to borrow money to buy a car, pay medical or tuition bills, or even fly down to DisneyWorld, he or she may be able to deduct the interest charged. Renters can deduct only a shrinking percentage of such interest, and by 1991, not a penny of that "consumer" or "personal" interest will be deductible. (For 1987, 65 percent of consumer interest was deductible; for 1988, 40 percent; for 1989, 20 percent; for 1990, 10 percent.)

That's not all. Tax-favored home owners may also (a) postpone paying capital-gains taxes on their profit when they sell their houses, or perhaps never have to pay any taxes on that profit; and/or (b) shield $125,000 worth of their profit from the IRS if they meet certain rules.

In sum, if you sincerely want to be rich (or just richer), thanks to the IRS, becoming a home owner is a pretty sure way to accomplish just that.

Yes, tax reform has shrunk some of the blessings of home ownership a bit.

With tax rates going down, deductions in general— such as for property taxes and for mortgage payments —aren't worth as much as they used to be. If you were in the 38.5 percent tax bracket in 1987, every additional $100 you paid for any deductible expenses wound up costing you merely $61.50. (You saved $38.50 on your taxes if you itemized.) In 1988 and thereafter, if you're in the 28 percent bracket, a deductible $100 expense will save you only $28, not $38.50.

Still, having some deductions is better than having no deductions.

Then too, the lenient treatment of long-term capital gains has flown the coop. (Long-term used to mean six months or more; beginning in 1987, it means a year or more.) For 1986, you had to pay taxes on only 40 percent of your long-term gains. In 1987, you wouldn't have to pay more than a 28 percent rate on your gains, even if you were in the 38.5 percent bracket. In 1988 and thereafter, long-term capital gains are being taxed just like your salary and other "ordinary" income—perhaps as high as 33 percent. That means home owners who can't shield their capital gains from

taxes will be socked harder than they were in the
past.

But remember: Home owners have special ways of
protecting their capital gains from being taxed. Those
twin blessings bestowed upon home owners—tax-de-
ferral and the one-time $125,000 exclusion—are
therefore worth more than ever.

Clearly, being a home owner—before and *after* tax
reform—is being on the good side of Uncle Sam.

Of course, don't buy a house if you can't really afford it—if your job isn't secure, or if you'll strip yourself bare of emergency money by making a down
payment. Other reasons to delay: You might have
more money available for a down payment next year,
and thus be able to wangle a mortgage at a lower interest rate by making a more hefty down payment. Or
you may think your local housing market is too high
and prices might come down.     *earthqk prices!*

But other things being equal, for tax reasons, buy a
house sooner rather than later.

First, we'll look at the tax advantages of buying a
residence, then the advantages (and disadvantages) of
borrowing on your house, and finally the advantages
when you sell.

## Tax Benefits When You Buy

You can begin deducting your property taxes and
mortgage interest *this* year if you buy a house now
rather than waiting. After all, the all-important rule
for lowering your taxes is: Defer income, and *take deductions now.*

You can also deduct any points you might pay to
obtain your mortgage. (Points are special up-front
charges that lenders may levy to lower the interest
rate on your mortgage.) Each point equals 1 percent of

your loan. If you take out a $50,000 mortgage and must pay 3 points, it's $1,500.

You can deduct these points all at once in the year you pay them if (a) you obtain a new mortgage (you don't refinance your old one); and (b) you pay the charges up front, all at once—you don't add the charges to your mortgage balance, paying them off over the life of your loan.

You must also segregate money you pay for points from other closing costs, like title insurance. Use a separate check.

## Home Equity Loans

What about borrowing on your house after you've lived there for a while?

Some young people—especially those with no financial background—may think that all deductions are desirable. They aren't. To get a deduction, you must spend (or lose) money. And if you don't spend your money wisely, the deduction you get is small solace.

Sure, you can deduct the cost of medical treatment by quacks (so long as they are licensed). You can deduct the mortgage interest you pay when you spring for a foolish home improvement—a gymnasium in a moderately priced house in a garden-variety community. You may be able to deduct the interest on a loan to buy commodities or other high-risk investments.

The point is: All deductions aren't desirable. And when you consider your *expenditure* minus the deduction, you're still out money.

But some deductible expenditures are wise, or necessary, or both. Borrowing money for certain home improvements, for example. Or to pay medical or educational expenses you couldn't pay otherwise. Or for a sound, well-researched investment.

Okay, you have a good reason to borrow money. Let's say you need a new car—your old one, which you use for work, has conked out. Or your house paint is peeling again, and you want your home covered with vinyl aluminum. In that case, the best way to borrow may be to use your house as collateral—to get a home equity loan. ("Equity" means what you own of the residence free and clear—subtracting mortgage debt from the current market value of your house.)

A home equity loan can be a second, or even a third, mortgage. But what it's come to mean is a home equity line of credit. You obtain access to a loan, secured by your home, whenever you need it. You don't pay any interest until you actually borrow the money, via a special credit card or a special check. And the interest you pay may be fully deductible—unlike interest you pay on loans *not* secured by your first or second residence.

If you're considering a home equity line of credit, first think about a straight second mortgage. Closing costs will be higher, but you can get a mortgage with a fixed interest rate. With most home equity lines of credit, you get a floating interest rate. (Fixed-rate home equity lines of credit are still rare.)

Also consider refinancing your old mortgage instead—especially if the interest rate you're paying is high.

And make sure you need the money in a home equity line of credit. It's all too easy to suddenly feel wealthy, and spend that money frivolously or recklessly.

Lenders keep urging people, "Unlock the money in your home!" Actually, you may be *endangering* the money in your home—money you may need for emergencies, money you may need for a comfortable retirement, money you may want to leave your children.

Some home owners have obtained home equity

lines of credit and used them as gigantic credit cards, buying expensive jewelry, vacation trips they cannot afford, and extravagant home improvements. Resolve not to get such a line of credit unless you have an excellent reason—and resolve not to spend anything beyond the amount you need.

Something else to consider: As the deductibility of consumer interest declines, a home equity line of credit will become more valuable in years to come. So it might be better to wait. On the other hand, there's lots of competition now, and now may be when you can get the best deal.

Before we get to the rules about deducting the interest on home equity loans, here's some advice about finding the best loan, courtesy of Anthony J. Mullen, a CPA in Drexel Hill, Pennsylvania:

- Look for a credit line with no fees of any kind— no closing costs and no bank charges.
- Try to get a fixed interest rate. Failing that, get a variable-rate loan, but with caps or limits.
- Look for a credit line that requires you to begin repaying the principal immediately. "I want to be *forced* to repay my balance," says Mullen. Some loans give you 10 years to repay your balance—or don't even set a time limit.
- Avoid one with a prepayment penalty. If the interest rate on a variable-rate loan climbs, you want to exit gracefully.
- Avoid one with ongoing fees—such as charges for checks, or a penalty for not using the credit that's available.

Don't assume that you can deduct all the interest on a home equity loan.

If you obtained a mortgage or line of credit, or refinanced your mortgage, after October 13, 1987, you must follow new rules beginning on your 1988 return (the one you fill out in 1989).

There will be a limit on fully deductible mortgage debt: the balance of your "acquisition" mortgage plus improvements plus $100,000. This means that any home owner can borrow at least $100,000 through a home equity loan, and deduct the interest in full, regardless of what the home cost originally—provided only that the total debt doesn't exceed the fair market value of the property.

And beginning on 1988 returns, there's a grandfather clause for mortgages obtained before October 14, 1987. All the debt will be treated as acquisition debt —and interest on up to $1 million is deductible.

## Refinancing Your Mortgage

As a rule, if current mortgage interest rates are 2 points below the rate you're paying now, and you plan on living in your home for at least a few years, it's probably worthwhile to get a new mortgage. First of all, you'll save on mortgage payments. And, second, assuming you refinance for more than your current mortgage balance, you will have more money at your disposal (because you will have paid off some of the principal, and your house has probably appreciated). The interest on the amount of your new mortgage will be fully deductible, provided that it's less than your house's original mortgage plus the cost of improvements plus $100,000 (if you refinanced after October 14, 1987).

## The Case for Not Selling

Once you sell your residence, to move into an apartment or another residence you don't own, you may owe taxes on any profits you've made from selling your homes.

So, apart from the fact that most people prefer living in their own homes, for tax reasons try to live in residences that you own. And try not to move often. If you move every few years, closing costs will cut down on, if not cancel out, your gains.

When you and your spouse die, your heirs will inherit the house without ever having to pay any taxes on the capital gains your house (or houses) have garnered over the years. (Death may be inevitable, but obviously that's not always true of taxes.) The other chief ways of reducing or eliminating capital-gains taxes on the sale of your residence follow.

## Reducing Taxes on Gains: Deferral

You can postpone (at least) paying taxes on the appreciation of your house when you sell it if:

1. You buy and live in another main home within two years after (or before) selling your old one. Yes, you can qualify even if you buy (or build) a new main home two years before selling your old one.
2. The new home is as expensive as or more expensive than the old one.
3. The homes you sold and bought are your main residences (not your summer homes). You could, of course, buy a second home in a resort area, use it as a vacation home for two years, then make it your main residence when you sell your other home.

You can use this deferral tactic over and over. But you cannot use it more than once every two years—

unless you move because of a job change and you fulfill the requirements to deduct the expenses on your tax return if you itemized your deductions.

The postponement of these taxes could come back to haunt you, though. The basis (cost for tax purposes) of your *new* house is lowered by whatever amount you avoided paying taxes on. If you avoided paying taxes on $20,000 of capital gains, then bought a $100,000 house, its basis would be only $80,000. That means that someday—when you sell that $100,000 house— you might have to pay taxes on that $20,000 profit. But you may be in a lower tax bracket when that day comes—and you'll have had all that extra time to use the money as you see fit. But remember that if you die while living in your main residence, the IRS will ignore all those capital gains.

What if you don't need a bigger house? How can you still buy a house at least as expensive and thus defer paying taxes on your gain? Buy a smaller house—but in a more expensive area. Or add improvements within two years of selling your old house, to bring the cost of your new house up to the sales price of your old one. Many people sell their homes when their kids move out, and buy a smaller place, but with larger grounds, just to have a more expensive house for tax purposes.

If your main dwelling is a trailer, houseboat, or yacht, it still qualifies for the deferral tactic— whether it's your old or your new residence. And your replacement residence doesn't even have to be in this country. In fact, if your home is outside the country— because, say, you're in the armed forces—you may have longer than two years to buy or build a replacement home.

If you must pay some capital gains taxes, you may have a choice about which gain to consider. Let's say

that you sell your house for $100,000. You have a
$20,000 gain. You buy another house for $90,000. Do
you owe taxes on the $20,000 gain—or on the $10,000
that cannot be deferred?

The IRS lets you choose the lower amount—in this
case, the $10,000 that cannot be deferred. The other
$10,000 is subtracted from the $90,000 to become the
tax basis of your new house: $80,000.

## Reducing Taxes on Gains: Boosting the Basis

Another way to lower your taxes is to raise your
house's basis—your total investment. Here's what you
can add to your purchase price:

- The cost of improvements. Examples are a new
  furnace, new carpeting, a new fence, central air-
  conditioning, new wiring or new plumbing. Repairs—such as patching your roof, or having a
  leaky pipe fixed—don't qualify. But *replacing*
  your roof does. (See page 163.) You can use the
  original cost of your improvements—even if you
  tacked down that carpeting years ago and it's
  rather tacky now. Don't count your own labor as
  part of the cost of an improvement. This is a good
  argument for letting someone else do it.
- Legal expenses connected with any improvements—such as your hiring a lawyer to get a
  variance (an exception to the planning code) so
  you could add an extra room.
- A real estate agent's fee, if you as a buyer used an
  agent (which is becoming more common).
- The cost of appliances you bought and left with
  the purchaser of your house, provided you didn't
  sell them separately from the house (room air
  conditioners, stove, microwave, and so forth).

- Closing costs, such as legal fees, recorder's fees, title insurance, and a termite inspection.
- Assessments for local improvements, such as new sidewalks or the widening of streets.

By the same token, you must lower your basis by casualty losses that you deducted in previous years (like a living room that was destroyed by fire); by residential energy credits you took (remember them?); and, of course, by any gains deferred from sales of your other houses.

Certain improvements don't add to the tax value of your house: the cost of removing structural barriers in a personal residence to make life easier for a handicapped person. But you can deduct the full cost when you pay for them, if they exceed 7.5 percent of your adjusted gross income. (You can also deduct operating expenses—the electricity that runs the air conditioner for your allergy, and the cost of having it repaired and maintained. The same goes for other doctor-recommended devices, like the cost of maintaining and running an elevator for a heart patient, or a special bath for an arthritis patient.)

These expenses to help the handicapped do *not* add to the value of your house, for tax purposes:

- Constructing entrance or exit ramps
- Widening doorways
- Modifying interior doorways and hallways to accommodate wheelchairs
- Installing railings and support bars in bathrooms, together with other similar changes
- Lowering kitchen cabinets and other equipment to make it easier for the handicapped to reach them
- Adjustment of electrical outlets and fixtures

As for other improvements made for medical reasons, you can deduct the cost from your income if you subtract the amount that such improvements added to the value of your house. (An appraiser can advise you.) Examples: swimming pools, air conditioners, central air-conditioning, home elevators or inclinators, and bedrooms and bathrooms added to a lower floor so that a patient doesn't have to do much stair climbing.

Make sure you don't forget any improvements that can raise your basis. You won't overlook major items such as an addition to your house, a new deck, or central air-conditioning. But don't forget new shelves, a repaved or widened driveway, new plants and bushes, wallpapering a room that had been painted. Go through your property, inside and outside, to refresh your memory.

Ideally, you'll have kept all your canceled checks, credit-card chits, and sales slips. If not, you may be able to get away with producing building permits for improvements, property-tax records, or before-and-after photographs of your house.

Still another way of lowering your gains: with moving expenses you couldn't deduct.

Now, you're better off itemizing your moving expenses, to get your deductions sooner. But if you can't itemize (because the sum of your deductions doesn't exceed the standard deduction), or you have reached the limits on your deductible moving expenses, add whatever expenses you can to the basis of your house or to the adjusted sales price.

## Reducing Taxes on Gains: Adjusting the Sales Price

Besides boosting your basis, you can lower whatever taxes you might owe by adjusting your sales price. (Not your real sales price—your price for tax purposes.) Here's what you can subtract to wind up with your "adjusted sales price":

- Real estate agent's commission.
- Legal fees, geological surveys, maps, termite inspections, and so forth.
- Any loan charges, such as points, that you as the seller must pay (if your buyer obtained, for example, a Veterans Administration-backed mortgage).
- The cost of advertising, for sale signs, and fact sheets if you sold your house yourself, without benefit of a broker. (You can deduct them even if you wound up having a broker sell your house.)
- Fix-up expenses for work performed during the 90 days before you sold your home, and paid for within 30 days after the sale. (The narrow time limit is to ensure that the expenses were truly to help you sell the house.) Examples: the cost of having the exterior or interior of your house painted, your plumbing repaired, new wallpaper installed. You can deduct fix-up costs only if you buy a less expensive house—because if you buy a house as expensive, you must defer the gains. So the fix-up costs wouldn't matter.

Here's an example of all these calculations, provided by the IRS:

Your selling expenses were $5,000. You spent $900 on new blinds and on a new water heater; you also spent $800 on painting your house—and met the rules regarding such fix-up expenses.

1. Selling price of old home: $61,400
2. Selling expenses: $5,000
3. Amount realized (1 minus 2): $56,400
4. Basis of old home: $45,000

5. Improvements (blinds, heater): $900
6. New basis of home (4 plus 5): $45,900
7. Gain on old home (3 minus 6): $10,500

You buy and live in another home costing $54,600, within two years of selling your old one. Now you can defer paying taxes on most of that $10,500.

8. Amount realized: $56,400
9. Fix-up expenses (painting): $800
10. Adjusted sales price (8 minus 9): $55,600
11. Cost of replacement home: $54,600
12. Gain *not* postponed (10 minus 11): $1,000
13. Gain postponed (7 minus 12): $9,500
14. Cost of new home: $54,600
15. Adjusted basis of new home (14 minus 13): $45,100

## Reducing Taxes on Gains: The $125,000 Exclusion

You can subtract $125,000 from your gains if (a) your house was your main residence, (b) you or your spouse were 55 when you sold the house (you didn't turn 55 at the end of that year) and owned it jointly, and (c) you or your spouse lived there for three of the five years before you sold it.

You can use this exclusion just once in your lifetime. But you can undo a mistake. Let's say that you use the exclusion to escape taxes on $20,000 of gain. You buy another house and, a few years later, you sell that one, for a $50,000 gain. You have three years from the date that your earlier return (with the smaller $20,000 exclusion) was due to be filed to cancel that first exclusion.

If you and your spouse owned the house jointly, and

your spouse was 55 or older, and had lived there for three of the past five years, you qualify for the exclusion—even if you're not 55, or hadn't lived in the house for three of the past five years.

Let's say you've never used the exclusion, and you're living in your own house. Now you plan to marry someone who *has* used the exclusion before, and you plan to live in your house when you marry. You'll be better off selling your house before you marry, or keeping the house in only your name. The fact that your new spouse has used the $125,000 exclusion would keep *you* from being able to use it—or even half of it.

Even if you rent out your house, you can still qualify for the $125,000 exclusion. But you must have rented the house for only two years, and lived there the previous three years.

## Deferral Versus Exclusion

Which is better—the deferral or the exclusion? Usually, the deferral. You can use it again and again. And, at a later time in your life, the exclusion may be more suitable, because you may want to live in a small house, or in an apartment. Also, your taxable gain may be higher later in life, because of the lowered basis of your last house, the result of all those deferrals.

Still, you may want to consider taking all of the $125,000 exclusion, *and* deferring the tax you owe on your remaining profit.

Here's an example, from the accounting firm of Seidman & Seidman/BDO:

You're 55, and sell your primary residence for $400,000. (Seidman & Seidman must have well-to-do clients!) The basis of your residence was $75,000.

1. Sales price of old home: $400,000
2. Tax basis of old home: $75,000
3. Gain (1 minus 2): $325,000
4. Exclusion: $125,000
5. Taxable gain (3 minus 4): $200,000

Now let's say that you buy a new house for $300,000. And now you can invoke the deferral tactic —even though your new house costs far less than your old one!

6. Sales price: $400,000
7. Exclusion: $125,000
8. New sales price (6 minus 7): $275,000
9. Price of new home: $300,000
10. Taxable gain (8 minus 9): 0
11. Tax basis of new home (9 minus 5): $100,000

## Deduct a Loss on Selling Your Home

...if you were renting it out. Some home owners who are selling for losses—typically because they bought a home in a deteriorating neighborhood, or where the main industry left—rent their houses for a few months, then try to deduct their loss. No good. You must prove to the IRS that you were renting the house for a profit, not just to deduct the loss on its sale. The longer you were renting it out, the more persuasive a case you can make. And you may need appraisals showing that the house had *not* declined in value before you began renting it out.

## Sell Your House to Your Kids

If you're getting on in years and need the money, sell your house to your children, in return for an annuity—a regular stream of payments for as long as you live. Otherwise, your house will be subject to estate taxes when you die, and your children's inheritance will shrink.

---

### Improvements Versus Repairs

Here's how the Internal Revenue Service explains the difference between improvements, which increase the tax basis of your home, and repairs, which do not:

**Improvements.** A home improvement materially adds to the value of your home, appreciably prolongs its useful life, or adapts it to new uses. Putting in a recreation room in your unfinished basement, adding another bathroom or bedroom, putting up a fence, putting in new plumbing or wiring, installing a new roof, or paving your driveway are improvements that are added to the basis of your home.

**Repairs.** A repair merely maintains your home in an ordinary, efficient operating condition. It doesn't add value to your home, or appreciably prolong its life. Repainting inside or outside, fixing your gutters or floors, mending leaks, and plastering and replacing broken windowpanes are examples of repairs.

# Index